Substance Abuse

SUBSTANCE ABUSE
A Resource Guide for Secondary Schools

Sally Myers and Blanche Woolls

1991
LIBRARIES UNLIMITED, INC.
Englewood, Colorado

LIBRARIES UNLIMITED, INC.
P.O. Box 3988
Englewood, CO 80155-3988

Library of Congress Cataloging-in-Publication Data

Myers, Sally.
Substance abuse : a resource guide for secondary schools / Sally Myers and Blanche Woolls.
xv, 167p. 17x25 cm.
Includes bibliographical references and index.
ISBN 0-87287-805-8
1. Substance abuse--United States--Bibliography. 2. Alcoholism--United States--Bibliography. 3. Drug abuse--United States--Bibliography. 4. Tobacco habit--United States--Bibliography. I. Woolls, Blanche. II. Title.
Z7164.S9M93 1991
[HV4999.2]
016.36229--dc20 90-24826
CIP

Contents

Acknowledgments

Many people have been helpful in the production of this volume, but three have been especially helpful—Mary Lou Ruddle, librarian at Carrick High School in Pittsburgh, and Todd Yeager and David McHenry, graduate assistants in the School of Library and Information Science, University of Pittsburgh. Mary Lou and her students previewed much of the media; and Todd found citations, wrote annotations, input data, and helped put it all together. Dave joined the project in the final stages and found every item or piece of data the rest of us had overlooked. After a first draft had been completed, additional films and videos were previewed by students in a school library management course.

Preface

The use and abuse of drugs began in ancient times, and the histories of various drugs may be found in sources cited in this bibliography. This bibliography is an update of three works by Theodora Andrews published by Libraries Unlimited. It is easy to build a case for providing new information targeting the secondary school audience.

When Andrews published her first bibliography in 1977, attention was focused on drugs with less emphasis on alcohol and tobacco. Her 1981 supplement showed that "some substances (notably marijuana) have been found to be more toxic than formerly presumed" and the increasing abuse of alcohol was emphasized. The preface to the third volume, published in 1985, states that "during the twentieth century, the only age group to show a rising death rate was Americans aged fifteen through twenty-four, who were dying at about a 15 percent higher rate in 1980 than in 1960 and that 30 percent of all Americans are now dying because of the use of alcohol and tobacco."[1]

On May 26, 1988, researchers reported before Sen. John Glenn's committee on government affairs that 10,600,000 Americans are alcoholics and that another 7,300,000 abuse drugs. Health officials believe that there are 5,000 new cocaine users daily and that 6,000,000 people are regular users with 200,000 to 1,000,000 of these compulsive users.[2] Many of these users are children and young adults under 18 years of age attending public and private schools in the United States today.

Statistics found in *Youth Indicators 1988*[3], published by the Office of Educational Research and Improvement of the U.S. Department of Education, indicate that the use (defined as having ever used) of heroin, LSD, and PCP is declining, alcohol usage by youth is stable at 91.3 percent, and use of marijuana and cocaine continues to rise. The number of students reported in the category "use of drugs in the past 12 months or the past 30 days" declined from 1975 to 1986 for marijuana and heroin use, but increased in use of cocaine.

Between 1983 and 1984, 35 percent of all public secondary schools reported that students had been caught selling illegal drugs at school. Of these, 31 percent were junior high and 39 percent were senior high. The incidence of students caught selling drugs at school is much higher in larger schools. Only 10 percent of the schools with less than 400 students were in that category, while 38 percent of those with a student body of 400 to 999 were in that category. When the school population increased to more than 1,000, the number of schools with students in this category increased to 63 percent.

Only 21 percent of rural schools had students who had been caught selling drugs while 46 percent of suburban schools and 51 percent of urban schools had students who had been caught selling drugs. Only 11 percent of the school districts with less than 1,000 population had students in this category while 40 percent of schools in districts with populations of 1,000 to 24,999 had students in this category. A total of 48 percent of the public school districts with more than 25,000 population had students caught selling illegal drugs at school. An alarming aspect of all these statistics is that, while students selling drugs are more often found in larger schools in urban areas, they are also found in smaller districts and in rural areas, areas many parents and teachers consider "safe" from the temptation of their more urban neighbors. The public considers the use of drugs as one of the chief problems facing local public schools, a rise of 11 percent of the respondents in 1970 to 30 percent in 1987.

Substance abuse continues to be a problem, and media specialists should be aware of sources of information for media center users. This volume is designed to provide literature on substance abuse for students who must conduct research and write reports on this topic and for teachers, administrators, and other educators who are concerned about the problems of substance abuse related to the students in their classrooms. It is hoped that parents will find the citations helpful as they seek information concerning this problem and how it relates to their children and their children's friends.

NOTES

[1]Theodora Andrews, *Substance Abuse Materials for School Libraries: An Annotated Bibliography* (Littleton, CO: Libraries Unlimited, 1985), ix.

[2]"Drugs Running the Numbers," *Research News* 240 (June 1988): 1729.

[3]*Youth Indicators 1988: Trends in the Well-Being of American Youth* (Washington, D.C.: U.S. Department of Education, 1988).

Introduction

Substance Abuse is intended to provide an introductory guide to resources and information on substance abuse. It covers such chemicals as alcohol, drugs, tobacco, and nicotine, which is included since it has been defined not only as a health hazard but also as a drug. This guide is designed to help users of the library collection find the historical background of substance abuse and to provide students and teachers with relevant facts about the dangers of drugs today. Books and audiovisual entries include titles appropriate for use by teachers and parents of secondary students and by the students themselves. Most of the materials listed have been reviewed by the authors, and the audiovisual materials have been viewed by students and school librarians. A copy of the evaluation form used is shown in appendix A. As a further help, the authors have located recommendations published in selected reviewing journals. When these were available, the name and date of the journal reviewing the item have been included at the close of the entry.

SELECTION OF ENTRIES

To select the potential entries, various subject headings were searched in many information sources including online databases of periodicals, research reports, and library media center holdings. Recent bibliographies were reviewed for inclusion of additional materials not previously cited. Journals published within the past five years reviewing secondary materials were searched to locate appropriate items. All the citations were checked against reviewing sources and the selection process began.

Once an item was thought to be appropriate for inclusion in this list, a copy was sought for review by the authors. An exhaustive search was made of secondary school, public, and special library collections to locate the items. When they were not available in local libraries, interlibrary loan requests were made. One book was sent to the authors from a school library in California, another from an academic library in Maine.

Selection Criteria

Materials entered into this bibliography meet the criteria usually applied to items for inclusion in any library collection:

1. cited as high quality in a review source
2. meeting a specific need in an area where little or no other materials are available
3. providing relevant, accurate information
4. in print at the time of development of the bibliography

Entries from the Andrews volumes have been reviewed for inclusion in this volume, new editions have been cited, prices have been updated, and items no longer in print have been excluded.

Library media specialists who wish to add materials on substance abuse to their collections should apply criteria from the selection policy in their school district. The importance of meeting curriculum needs in this area is high priority. Teachers and students need accurate information presented in a relevant and interesting manner and format. This particular area might lend itself to heavy scrutiny by activist groups hoping to impose their selection criteria on the school. The criteria used for inclusion of materials found in the media specialist's own selection policy will support collection decisions. Media specialists and librarians in public libraries are reminded that selection policies approved by the school board or other governing authority are essential if censors are to be answered in a positive manner.

A SEARCHER'S GUIDE TO SUBSTANCE ABUSE

The headings listed below have been included for readers unfamiliar with terminology used in classifying and indexing and who wish to locate additional items.

Library of Congress Headings

Library of Congress subject headings are used for entry in the card catalog or in the online public access catalog of most public and academic libraries. It is the subject heading list used in Pennsylvania for entries onto the Access Pennsylvania CD-ROM database, a source for this bibliography, which includes more than 2 million titles and 6 million volumes. Searches might include headings such as substance abuse, aerosol sniffing, alcoholism, caffeine habit, drug abuse, solvent abuse, and tobacco habit. A more complete list of search terms may be found in appendix B.

Readers' Guide to Periodical Literature

For searchers interested in magazine articles, headings in *Readers' Guide to Periodical Literature* would include:

Alcoholics and alcoholism	Drugs and youth
Children of drug addicts	Drug education
Cocaine	Heroin
Crack (cocaine)	Marijuana
Chewing tocacco	Nicotine
Drug abuse	Smokeless tobacco
Drugs and celebrities	Smoking
Drugs and crime	Smoking and employment
Drugs and the press	Smoking and youth
Drugs and sports	Smoking on airplanes
Drugs and women	Tobacco

To use the *Readers' Guide*, look up the last subject heading on this list, "smoking." Note that "smoking" appears in all capital letters and in bold face type. Not only is the subject found, but also MATCHCOVERS & SMOKENDERS (Organization). These are additional subject headings or places to look in the *Readers' Guide*. They would broaden your search.

Thesaurus of ERIC Descriptors, 11th edition (1987)

Descriptors in this volume that are related to substance abuse include the following:

Alcohol Education	Food & Drug Inspectors
Alcoholic Beverages	Illegal Drug Use
Alcoholism	Marijuana
Drinking	Sedatives
Drug Abuse	Special Health Problems
Drug Addiction	Tobacco
Drug Education	
Drug Legislation	Transferred descriptors still searchable: Marihuana
Drug Rehabilitation	
Drug Therapy	
Drug Use	

Online Databases

Many media specialists have access to online databases in their media centers or may use the online services of the local public library or nearby university. The economy of CD-ROM databases has also made this form of information appealing to even the smallest school library media center. A sample BRS search and output are provided in appendix C.

FORMAT FOR THE VOLUME

This book is divided into several collections: the general collection (the primary entry point), reference materials, a section listing information specifically for educators (teachers and administrators), and one for parents. Free and inexpensive materials, such as pamphlets, are included in a special section.

The general list contains all types of materials in a variety of formats. The format has been indicated. Abbreviations in the left-hand margin indicate the type of material for the following:

F / Fiction	FLM / Film
NF / Nonfiction	VHS / Video
FS / Filmstrip	DSK / Computer disk

Sources were placed in reference rather than the general list when they provided brief, immediate responses to queries or offered guides to additional locations for information. Therefore, dictionaries, bibliographies, and encyclopedias are included as well as databases and periodicals featuring substance abuse information. Basic reference tools that have annual statistical updates such as *Statistical Abstracts* are listed.

If an entry would be of interest to teachers, administrators, or parents, the bibliographic citation is given in that section with a note guiding the reader to the general collection for annotations and any reviews found for that title.

ACCESS TO GOVERNMENT PUBLICATIONS

Government publications offer an excellent, inexpensive, and timely source of information on substance abuse. The difficulty of locating these publications may have caused the authors to miss excellent sources. As an aid to the reader, here are some suggestions for locating additional materials which will become available at intervals.

The three pertinent agencies producing this material are The National Institute on Alcohol Abuse and Alcoholism, The National Institute on Drug Abuse, and The National Institute of Mental Health. Access to these publications is through the Government Printing Office and its *Monthly Catalog of U.S. Government Publications.*

The *Monthly Catalog* is available in print, online, and as a CD-ROM; Government Printing Office (GPO) cataloging is also available through the OCLC database. Assistance in using the *Monthly Catalog* is given at your nearest depository library. A list of depository libraries can be secured from the Government Printing Office, Superintendent of Documents, Washington, D.C. 20402, or from the twenty-four federal bookstores in major cities.

This is a current bibliography of publications issued to all branches of the government, including congressional as well as the department and bureau publications that are printed by the Government Printing Offices and distributed by the Superintendent of Documents. Arrangement is by issuing agency with monthly indexes cumulated annually. An additional aid to subject retrieval is the *Cumulative Subject Index to the Monthly Catalog of U.S. Government Publications, 1900-1971*. It is compiled by William W. Buchanan and Edna M. Kanely (Washington, D.C.: Carrolton Press, 1973-1975. 15 vol.) Each issue of the catalog contains general information and instructions for ordering documents.

United States documents constitute a complex field, and the *Monthly Catalog* is not a complete listing of materials. It does not include certain publications, such as those published directly by the issuing agency or those contracted for by government agencies. However, it is important because a great deal of drug abuse material is included. Since much in this field is published by various government agencies, a large portion of it is suitable for laypersons.

The National Clearinghouse for Alcohol and Drug Information, Box 2345, Rockville, MD 20852 maintains mailing lists for free publications. Writing to this agency will place your library's name on their mailing list and you will receive regular announcements and publications. Additionally, some government publications on substance abuse are available from the Consumer Information Center, P.O. Box 100, Pueblo, CO 81002.

A final four appendixes provide additional resources for the information searcher. Appendix E includes the complete text of an article by Zigmond A. Kozicki that provides some explanation for substance abuse by adolescents. A list of state agencies is given. This list is provided in many of the entries in the general collection but is repeated here for instant reference. An order form for Al-Anon pamphlets is reproduced in appendix G. Appendix H includes drug abuse curricula for teachers and the media specialist.

FORMAT OF ENTRIES

The format for each entry includes author, title, publisher, date, notes such as bibliog. or illus., number of pages/disks/frames. The cost of the item is followed by the Library of Congress number and the ISBN when they were available. When an entry has been reviewed in a journal, the name of the journal and the date of issue are cited. The recommended grade level is provided when possible.

As mentioned previously, citations were checked in indexes to book reviews and other types of media. When reviews were found, the reviewing source is cited to help school library media specialists whose selection policies suggest that they use reviewing journals to help select materials.

1

The General Collection
Print and Nonprint

This section contains materials for use by a wide audience including students as well as teachers, parents, and administrators. The list is all-inclusive.

Reference materials and materials specifically designed for parents and administrators are featured in separate chapters following this general collection. Some titles in the general collection might just as appropriately be considered reference works; it was the authors' discretion to place them in the general collection. Since these items are suitable for educating about substance abuse, for sharing information with adults and students, or for student research papers, they have been judged "general." Bibliographic entries may be repeated for materials appropriate for administrators or parents, but the complete annotation is found in this section.

Three "encyclopedias" are listed here, but they are not true encyclopedic references. Each volume is on a separate topic and by separate authors; they are included by author and annotated individually. The first two encyclopedias are Snyder, Solomon, eds. *Encyclopedia of Psychoactive Drugs* and Snyder, Solomon, eds. *Encyclopedia of Psychoactive Drugs Series 2.* The *Encyclopedia of Psychoactive Drugs* is an authoritative source of drug information for young adults and adults in general. The editors' aim is to answer questions likely to be asked about drugs and other questions young adults might not think to ask. The format is clear, authoritative, and concise. All volumes are handsomely and appropriately illustrated. While volumes may have duplicate introductions, the appendixes differ, and for this reason they have been reported.

The last encyclopedia is *The Encyclopedia of Health Series*, an ongoing series divided into four areas: the life cycle, medical disorders and treatments, medical issues, and wellness. Each book has the same introduction. Since not all of the volumes cover substance abuse, only those directly related to this topic are included here.

VHS
Adult Children of Alcoholics. Richard Robertson (producer) for Hospital Satellite Network. Van Nuys, CA: AIMS Media, 1988. 28 min. video. $295.00. (GR 9-adult)

Children who grow up in a family where one or both parents are alcoholics often have difficulties facing the world and people in it. This video presents twelve steps designed by Alcoholics Anonymous as an effective treatment for the psychological problems of adult children of alcoholics who suffer from stress disorders, codependence, and lack of social skills, among others.

Reviewed in *Booklist*, August 1989; *Library Journal*, July 1989.

FIC
Alcock, Vivien. **The Trial of Anna Cotman**. New York: Delacorte, 1990. 60p. $13.95. LC 89-23302. ISBN 0-385-29981-8. (GR 6-10)

Anna finds friendship in a masked, secret society that meets in a cellar. The rules and rituals of the secret gang become more and more cruel as the story progresses until the gang leader, the brother of Anna's friend, Lindy, is shown to be a drug addict. At this time Lindy's stepfather sends the brother for treatment.

Reviewed in *Booklist*, January 1, 1990.

DSK
Alcohol. Portland, OR: Student Awareness, 1988. $45.00. 4 interactive programs for the IBM or compatible. (GR 7-12)

This computer program includes four double-sided disks and a teacher disk. The format is question-and-answer under titles including "Alcohol: Your Health," "Drinking Risks: Decisions," "Drinking, Driving & You," "Questions, Myths: Answers."

VHS
Alcohol Addiction. Princeton, NJ: Films for Humanities, 1988. 28 min. video. $149.00; $199.00, ¾". (GR 10-12)

Bill Moyers is host to this program on genetic susceptibility, access, and attitude as they relate to alcohol addiction. Interviews with scientists help to explain why one person can be a social drinker when another will become an alcoholic. The video concludes with the director of an institution for persons undergoing addictive behavior therapy, who explains that persons wishing to change their alcoholic abuse must change their lifestyles.

Reviewed in *School Library Journal*, May 1989.

FLM/VHS
Alcohol Addiction and Teens. Producer and director: Richard Gerdau. Van Nuys, CA: AIMS Media, 1987. 14 min. (ABC News "Closeups"). guide. film and video. $330.00; $275.00. LC 88-709406; LC 88-709407.

The use of alcohol among teens and how this affects their families is the subject of this film. The brain maps of two teenagers are compared to illustrate the differences in emotions and memory when alcoholism of a parent is present in the home.

Reviewed in *Booklist*, August 1988.

VHS
Alcohol, Children, and the Family. Distributed by: Hospital Satellite Network. Van Nuys, CA: AIMS Media, 1988. 20 min. video. $295.00. (GR 9-adult)

Children with one or two alcoholic parents grow up to have social and other psychological problems as adults. This film addresses this problem.

Reviewed in *School Library Journal*, July 1989.

FLM/VHS
Alcohol & Cocaine. Producer and director: Richard Gerdau. Van Nuys, CA: AIMS Media, 1987. 36 min. guide. film, $545.00; video, $395.00. LC 88-709405; LC 88-707118.

This documentary and interviews with scientists and recovering addicts explores addiction. Genetics is explained as a reason some persons are more susceptible than others, and the physical damage to the body is presented as it relates to hormones of the body, the brain, and body cells.

Reviewed in *Booklist*, August 1988.

NF
Alcohol and Health: Seventh Special Report to the U.S. Congress from the Secretary of Health & Human Services, January, 1990. Washington, D.C.: U.S. Department of Health and Human Services, Public Health Service, 1990. 189p. Free.

Topics include alcohol abuse and alcoholism; epidemiology, genetics, and environment; neuroscience; medical consequences; fetal alcohol syndrome and other effects of alcohol on pregnancy; adverse social consequences; diagnosis and assessment of alcohol use; disorders; prevention; early and minimal intervention; and treatment.

FS
Alcoholism: Who Pays the Tab? Ridgefield, CT: Current Affairs, 1980. Enhancell Video. $39.95.

The costs of alcoholism are obviously enormous—not only economic costs but the human costs of individual suffering, wasted potential, and lost lives. Also, during the past decade, the number of teenage alcoholics has risen considerably. This sound filmstrip surveys the problem and its costs in an open-ended fashion designed to motivate viewer discussion.

NF
Al-Anon Family Group Headquarters, Inc. **Alateen—Hope for Children of Alcoholics.** New York: Al-Anon Family Group Headquarters, 1986. $4.00. 114p. LC 73-82710. ISBN 0-910-03420-6.

Alateen groups (for persons aged twelve to twenty) are sponsored by Al-Anon members. Both groups are outgrowths of Alcoholics Anonymous and are designed to support the family or friends of an alcoholic whether or not the alcoholic is seeking help.

This handbook provides information on organizing an Alateen group and tells how to plan a meeting. Also included are personal narratives which tell you how young persons have learned to cope with an alcoholic parent. Alateen's philosophy and the "twelve steps" are explained. These, as in Alcoholics Anonymous, involve belief in God and acceptance of the alcoholic's problems.

NF

Allen, William A., Nicholas L. Piccone, and Christopher D'Amanada. **How Drugs Can Affect Your Life: The Effects of Drugs on Safety and Well-Being—With Emphasis on Prevention of Drug Use.** 2d ed. Springfield, IL: Charles C. Thomas, 1987. illus. bibliog. index. 235p. $23.50. LC 87-10119. ISBN 0-398-05370-7.

A wide variety of subjects in the drug and alcohol abuse field are covered in this work. It was written to assist young people and their parents in dealing with substance abuse. It especially provides information that should help youths resist arguments for using drugs by presenting a convincing case against drugs. Chapter titles include "How It All Began—Drugs, Alcohol, Smoking," "What Drugs Are All About," "How Drugs Affect Mind and Body," "Changes in Life-Style and Other Drug Effects," "Fetal Alcohol Syndrome—What It Does to Children," "Drugs and Sexuality," "Prevention—For Parents, Teachers, Youths, and Others," "Drugs and Driving," "Drug Highs Versus Natural Highs," "Drugs and the Law," "Dealing with Drug Overdose," "Where to Turn for Help—Resources in Your Community," "The Great Addicter— Cocaine," and "AIDS." The 93-item bibliography contains newspaper and magazine articles as well as books.

NF

Alpert, Janice. **The I-Quit-Smoking Diet: The Revolutionary 21-Day Plan That Lets You Stop Smoking Without Gaining Weight.** Chicago: Contemporary Books, 1988. bibliog. charts. 123p. $16.95. LC 88-11718. ISBN 0-8092-4587-6.

Designed to help the reader lose weight, this book also describes the behavior leading to the craving for tobacco that would lead to craving for food. A twenty-one-day menu with accompanying recipes includes potato chips and ice cream. The need for exercise is also stressed.

Reviewed in *Booklist*, June 15, 1988.

NF

Arkaua, Morton L., and John E. Russell. **Coping with Smoking.** New York: Rosen, 1984. 132p. index. illus. $12.95. LC 83-24581. ISBN 0-8239-0614-0.

This very small book contains information about the history of tobacco use, why people start smoking, asserting your rights as a nonsmoker, resisting the pressure of friends to smoke, mutual aid programs, why it is difficult to quit, choices for the smoker, and ten steps to quitting. The chapter on "Where to Get Help to Quit" contains names, addresses, and brief descriptions of nine agencies. Further, there are toll-free "800" numbers provided by the National Cancer Institute for twenty-nine states and the District of Columbia, plus one "for all other states." The final chapter suggests that quitting is easier when you "help yourself by helping others."

NF

August, Paul Nordstrom. **Drugs and Women.** New York: Chelsea House, 1987. 119p. illus. (The Encyclopedia of Psychoactive Drugs) $17.95. LC 86-34346. ISBN 1-555-46227-8.

This volume details the increased use of drugs among women at the present time. The effects of drugs, both legal and illicit, are stated, and the sociological and cultural reasons for drug use by women are discussed. Chapter titles include "Social and Cultural Factors," "Women and Alcohol," "Women and Cigarettes," "Women and Stimulants," "Women and Depressants," "Women and Marijuana," "Women and Opiates," "Drugs and Reproduction," and "A Note to Teenage Readers." The appendix includes state agencies for the prevention and treatment of drug abuse and a glossary with sixty-two terms.

NF
Avraham, Regina. **The Downside of Drugs.** New York: Chelsea House, 1988. 110p. illus. photos. (The Encyclopedia of Psychoactive Drugs) $17.95. LC 87-26782. ISBN 1-555-46234.

This book "seeks to explain how various substances can cause physical and emotional complications in a user's life." Chapters are "Nicotine: The Most Addictive Drug," "Alcohol," "Narcotics," "Stimulants: Amphetamines and Cocaine," "Depressants: Barbiturates and Tranquilizers," "Hallucinogens: The Psychedelic Drugs," and "The New Drugs: Today and Tomorrow." Appendix includes state agencies for the prevention and treatment of drug abuse, an eleven-item bibliography, and a glossary of thirty-nine terms.

NF
Avraham, Regina. **Prescription & Over-the-Counter Drugs.** New York: Chelsea House, 1989. 110p. (The Encyclopedia of Health Series) $17.95. ISBN 0-7910-00062-1. (GR 7-12)

This book presents both the good and bad sides of these drugs.

Reviewed in *Book Report*, November-December 1989.

NF
Avraham, Regina. **Substance Abuse; Prevention and Treatment.** New York: Chelsea House, 1986. 128p. illus. photos. (The Encyclopedia of Psychoactive Drugs) $17.95. LC 88-4297. ISBN 1-555-46219-7.

The caption under one of the photographs in this volume states, "The United States is a market for more than two-thirds of the world's supply of cocaine." Chapters include "Attempts at Prevention and Control," "The Nature of Drug Addiction," "Treating Drug Abuse," "Addiction and the Family," "Alcoholism," "Methadone Maintenance," "A Look at Treatment Centers," and "The Bottom Line." The appendix includes state agencies for the prevention and treatment of drug abuse, twelve items for further reading, and a glossary of twenty-nine terms.

NF
Babor, Thomas. **Alcohol: Customs and Rituals.** New York: Chelsea House, 1986. 125p. illus. (The Encyclopedia of Psychoactive Drugs) $17.95. LC 85-17466. ISBN 0-877-54763-7.

A very thorough treatment of current topics in alcohol and alcoholism. The book, which makes very effective use of pictures and charts, covers the history of alcohol use; changing attitudes toward alcoholism; properties and effects of alcohol; use and abuse of alcohol; and prevention, intervention, and treatment. Chapter titles include "Drinking Throughout the Ages," "Drinking in the United States," "Drinking Around the World," "Drinking in Latin America, Africa, Asia," and "Drinking in the 1980's." The appendix includes state agencies for the prevention and treatment of drug abuse.

NF
Bach, Julie S., Ed. **Drug Abuse.** San Diego, CA: Greenhaven Press, 1987. 212p. charts. diagrams. bibliog. index. illus. (Opposing Viewpoint Series) $13.95; $6.95 pa. LC 87-14837. ISBN 0-89908-401-X. (GR 8-up)

A collection of articles from popular magazines, this book provides discussion on the pros and cons of steroids, marijuana, prescription drug dispensing, and mandatory drug testing. Chapter titles include "How Should the War on Drugs Be Waged?", "Are International Drug Campaigns Effective?", "Should Drug Testing Be Used?", "What Should Be Done About the Drug Problem in Sports?", and "How Should Drugs Be Legally Prescribed?" A variety of viewpoints including religious, political, and moral are given. Illustrated with political cartoons, this volume contains a list of organizations that help with drug abuse and bibliographies of periodicals.

Reviewed in *Booklist*, December 1, 1987 and *School Library Journal*, February 1988.

VHS
Back to Reality. Minneapolis, MN: The Johnson Institute, 1989. 31 min. Video. $565.00. Facilitator's Guide.

Narrated by Hugh Downs, this is the first in a three-part video series including *Enabling: Masking Reality and Intervention* and *Intervention: Facing Reality*, cited elsewhere. Through real-life scenes, this video describes what addiction is, how it affects addicts, how it affects those around them, where it leads, and what can be done about it.

NF
Backer, Thomas E. **Strategic Planning for Workplace Drug Abuse Programs.** Rockville, MD: Office for Research Communications, National Institute on Drug Abuse, [1987]. DHHS Pub. No. (ADM) 87-1537.

The introduction to this government publication states that "The American economy suffers billions of dollars in losses attributable to drug abuse each year." Chapters include "The Challenge," "The Response," "Planning for a Workplace Drug Abuse Program," "Implementing a Drug Abuse Program," "Special Issues," and "Model Programs." The bibliography is divided into general references, references on drug abuse and the workplace, employee assistance programs, drug policy, drug testing, and strategic planning. The appendix includes selected annotated references to twelve sources that would provide a "short course on workplace drug abuse programs," sample policy statements, sample management training approaches, and state drug abuse authorities. A final listing of resources includes audiovisual and multimedia packages, periodicals, and organizations.

NF
Bakalar, James B., and Lester Grinspoon. **Drug Control in a Free Society.** New York: Cambridge University Press, 1985. 174p. $29.95; $10.95 pa. LC 84-11347. ISBN 0-52135-772-1.

Techniques to alter consciousness have been known to man for hundreds of years. Alcohol and drugs are the most prominent in today's society. This book is an analysis of the philosophical, sociological, legal, moral, political, and historical background for controlling drugs that alter consciousness in today's industrial society. The debate is between the individual's right to experiment and the government's right to protect the citizens.

Reviewed in *Choice*, October 1985, and *Contemporary Psychology*, June 1986.

NF

Beattie, Melody. **Beyond Codependency: And Getting Better All the Time.** New York: Harper & Row, 1989. 240p. bibliog. $9.95 pa. LC 88-45986. ISBN 0-06-255418-2.

Persons who have let another's behavior affect them and have tried to help by controlling that behavior are described as "codependent" by the author of this book. This book suggests that codependency goes beyond parents or spouses of substance abusers and includes friends. The author includes the typical topics and also includes the process of continuing a treatment process once it has started.

Reviewed in *Library Journal*, July 1989.

NF

Benner, Janet. **Smoking Cigarettes: The Unfiltered Truth.** Santa Barbara, CA: Joelle Publishing, 1987. 142p. bibliog. index. $10.95. LC 87-80270. ISBN 0-942723-12-7. (YA)

While this book is designed for the smoker who wishes to quit smoking, it is not a specific plan to do so. Rather it is a collection of data on the physical effects of the habit with a collection of strategies that might be employed. Smokers who have overcome the habit provide suggestions for quitting cigarettes. Historical and legal information as well as technological advances that might be used are included.

Reviewed in *Booklist*, December 15, 1987.

NF

Berger, Gilda. **Crack, the New Drug Epidemic.** New York: Watts, 1987. 128p. $11.90. LC 87-6119. ISBN 0-531-10410-9. (GR 7-10)

Comprehensive treatment of the crack problem in the United States by an author who has written several books on addiction. Since teenagers have become one of the largest markets for this deadly new drug, this book discusses the reasons behind the popularity of crack. Included are easily understandable descriptions of crack, its producers, its users, its dangers, manufacture, and efforts to stop it, as well as care and treatment of crack addicts. The basic arguments for strict laws and drug-testing procedures are given. Black and white photographs, glossary, reading list, index, and illustrations.

Reviewed in *Booklist*, December 15, 1987.

NF

Berger, Gilda. **Drug Abuse: The Impact on Society.** New York: Watts, 1988. 144p. $12.90. LC 88-10620. ISBN 0-531-10579-2.

The book begins with the story of Peter, who is seventeen, lives at home, and has been smoking and drinking beer since he was ten years old. At thirteen he was smoking joints of marijuana, and at fifteen he began doing drugs every day. This scenario then makes the premise that substance abusers hurt themselves and others through their abuse of drugs even as they say "It's no one's business. What difference is it to you if I do drugs?" The author's premise is that an individual cannot stop the supply of drugs, but each one can prevent drug use for oneself and the people around one by learning about the impact of drugs. Black and white photographs are interspersed throughout the text. Chapter titles include "The Social History of Drugs," "The Illegal Drugs," "Health and Personality Effects," "AIDS," "Street Crime," "Drug Dealing," "Drug Trafficking," "Toll on the Family," "Drugs in the Workplace," "Drugs and Role Models," and "Ethical Issues."

NF
Berger, Gilda. **Drug Testing: A New Weapon to Fight the Drug Crisis.** New York: Watts, 1987. 128p. illus. (An Impact Book) $11.90. LC 87-13369. ISBN 0-531-10411-7.

Drug testing has become an issue of growing concern and controversy. Gilda Berger explores the civil rights issues involved in the drug problem and the tests themselves (methodology, reliability, and other matters). Legal and ethical issues are also presented in various environments: schools, professional sports, the military, private industry, and the public sector. She explains how drug tests are conducted and their effectiveness as well as the positive and negative aspects of their use. This book has some black and white photographs as illustrations.

Reviewed in *Booklist*, December 15, 1987.

NF
Berger, Gilda. **Making Up Your Mind about Drugs.** New York: Lodestar Books, 1988. 80p. $10.95. LC 88-10575. ISBN 0-525-67251-6. (GR 3-8)

Designed for a younger reader, the book would be useful for junior high as well. The author explains the facts about drugs and how they affect the body. Not only does the author discuss the choice of whether or not to use drugs, she offers alternatives to getting high.

Reviewed in *Wilson Library Bulletin*, May 1989.

NF
Berger, Gilda. **Smoking Not Allowed.** New York: Watts, 1987. 144p. index. illus. $11.90. LC 87-10575. ISBN 0-531-10420-6. (GR 7-9)

The prolific Gilda Berger sheds some fresh light on this 400-year-old controversy as she traces the history of smoking through all its forms and eras of favor and disfavor in part 1. Part II explores the issues: health effects and social, economic, and legal aspects. Appendixes cite further reading.

NF
Beschner, George, and Alfred S. Friedman. **Teen Drug Use.** Lexington, MA: Lexington Books, 1986. 243p. index. bibliog. $14.95 pa. LC 85-45378. ISBN 0-669-13834-7.

In a very personal way, this book traces the tragedy of teen drug addiction through its progressive phases: getting acquainted, the start, the first time, the addiction, the last straw, the beginning, and the road back. Firmly grounded in realism, the text follows the case study of a real addict progressing through these stages. As with other books in this series, a list of help agencies is included.

NF

Bevan, Nicholas. **AIDS and Drugs.** New York: Watts, 1988. 62p. index. diagrams. glossary. photos. (Understanding Drugs Series) $11.90. LC 88-50495. ISBN 053-10625-X. (GR 6 and up)

The relationship between drugs and AIDS, that between AIDS and sex, the origins of AIDS, and medical drugs used in the treatment of this disease are presented in this book.

NF

Brecher, Edward M., and the Editors of Consumer Reports. **Licit and Illicit Drugs: The Consumers Union Report on Narcotics, Stimulants, Depressants, Inhalants, Hallucinogens, and Marijuana—Including Caffeine, Nicotine, and Alcohol.** Boston: Little, Brown, and Co., 1972. 623p. bibliog. index. $13.95. LC 75-186972. ISBN 0-316-15340-0.

This report was undertaken because the editors felt that the illicit drug scene in the U.S. was becoming intolerable. All aspects of drug abuse are taken up—the pharmacology, the effects of drug laws, drug policies, and drug attitudes. Each drug is presented in historical perspective. It is interesting to note that the "licit" drugs referred to are caffeine, nicotine, and alcohol; many readers may feel that caffeine and nicotine are not quite in the same class as alcohol.

The work is well documented and thorough. It ends with recommendations that the authors hoped would point the way to both short-term and long-term improvements in the critical situation. The authors did not claim that the recommendations constituted a panacea, yet many readers felt that implementing them would not improve matters at all, and perhaps would make them worse. The primary recommendation was that marijuana use should be made legal, but subject to regulation. Although the book was widely sold and is still read, it is not current now. Much of what is known about the effects of drug abuse has been discovered recently.

FIC

Brooks, Bruce. **No Kidding.** New York: Harper, 1989. 207p. $13.89. LC 88-22057. ISBN 0-06-020723-X. (GR 9-12)

In the next century, the only disease in the world is alcoholism, and almost 70 percent of the adult population is alcoholic. The hero, Sam, tries to bring his family together. His father has departed to become a minister, so Sam, an adult at 14, sends his mother for treatment. His younger brother is placed in a foster home. Sam must decide whether to return his brother to his mother or allow him to be adopted by the foster family. This story does not have a happy ending.

Reviewed in *Book Report*, November/December 1989.

NF

Browne, David. **Crack and Cocaine.** New York: Gloucester Press (Watts), 1987. 32p. illus. $10.90. LC 86-83110. ISBN 0-531-17047-0. (GR 5-8)

A brief overview of the growing problem of cocaine abuse in the United States with emphasis on the powerful, extremely addictive form known as "crack." The format of the book is oversize with many black-and-white photographs as well as definitions for the more difficult words, and this may increase its in-library use. The introduction portrays a crack house as "a modern day opium den." Included are descriptions of cocaine smuggling into the United States, drug dealers who reap their fortunes from illegal drug sales, and children and workers who are daily drug users. Addresses and telephone numbers for agencies including the National Cocaine Hotline are given in the final chapter.

Reviewed in *Booklist*, June 1, 1987, and *School Library Journal*, August 1987.

FIC

Butterworth, W. E. **Under the Influence.** New York: Four Winds Press, 1979. 256p. $9.95. LC 78-22127. ISBN 0-02-716240-0.

This is a novel about two young high school boys who become great friends. As the friendship develops, Allan, the youth who tells the story, realizes that his friend is an alcoholic whose behavior is jeopardizing himself and others. Allan attempts to be loyal, in spite of the trouble his friend makes.

In the final chapter the alcoholic youth has a mental collapse from which he may never recover because of guilt about a death he is responsible for. Although the tragedy touches virtually all the characters in the book, Allan, his girlfriend, and his family maintain satisfactory relationships.

NF

Byck, Robert. **Treating Mental Illness.** New York: Chelsea House, 1986. 91p. illus. (The Encyclopedia of Psychoactive Drugs) $17.95. LC 85-32564. ISBN 0-877-54774-2.

Mood-modifying drugs are often used to correct chemical imbalances in the brain that are believed to cause mental illnesses such as depression and schizophrenia. Chapter titles include "Antipsychotic Drugs," "Depression," "Manic-Depressive Psychosis," and "The Future." The appendix includes "Symptoms of Clinical Depression," "Symptoms of Mania," "Symptoms of Schizophrenia," state agencies for the prevention and treatment of drug abuse, and a glossary of 66 terms.

NF

Carroll, Marilyn. **PCP: The Dangerous Angel.** New York: Chelsea House, 1985. 110p. illus. (The Encyclopedia of Psychoactive Drugs) $17.95. LC 85-3730. ISBN 0-877-54753-X.

The chemical properties of phencyclidine (PCP) are described. This hallucinogen, originally used as a pre-surgery anesthetic, is shown to have severe physical and psychological effects that can cause serious mental illness and even death. The short- and long-term effects, tolerance, dependence, treatment, and uses are described. The low cost of chemicals needed to make PCP and the ease of mixing make this an easy drug to manufacture. The final chapter points out the legal ramifications of producing PCP as well as the relationship of PCP to crime. Appendixes include a list of state agencies for the prevention and treatment of drug abuse, a short bibliography, and a glossary of 64 terms.

One reviewer of this book suggests that the date be noted. With a 1985 copyright, information is becoming outdated. The book will be popular with students because it is written in easy-to-read language with many charts and pictures.

NF

Carroll, Marilyn, and Gary Gallo. **Quaaludes: the Quest for Oblivion.** New York: Chelsea House, 1985. 104p. illus. (The Encyclopedia of Psychoactive Drugs) $17.95. LC 85-11043. ISBN 0-877-54753-X.

This is a description of the nature, effects, and medical and legal aspects of methaqualone use and abuse. Chapter titles include "What Is Methaqualone?," "The Short-Term Effects of Methaqualone," "The Effects of Chronic Methaqualone Use," "Medical Treatment for Methaqualone Abuse," "Methaqualone and Other Drugs," and "The Extent of Methaqualone Use." The appendix includes a glossary with 38 terms and list of state agencies for the prevention and treatment of drug abuse.

FIC

Carter, Alden R. **Up Country.** New York: Putnam, 1989. 256p. $15.95. LC 88-37959. ISBN 0-399-21583-2. (GR 6-10)

Carl, age 16, is a straight-A student with a talent for electronics. He lives in a basement to hide from his alcoholic mother and her variety of friends, planning to repair stolen car stereos to earn enough money to go to college. When his mother is arrested for drunken hit-and-run driving and sent to a detoxification center, Carl is sent from Milwaukee to rural Wisconsin to live with his aunt, uncle, and cousin. As Carl begins to adjust to the new environment and finds a new girlfriend, his relationship to the stereo thieves is discovered. The novel manages to escape being didactic.

Reviewed in *Book Report*, November/December 1989; *Booklist*, July 1989; and *School Library Journal*, June 1989.

NF

Check, William A. **Drugs and Perception.** New York: Chelsea House, 1988. 112p. illus. (The Encyclopedia of Psychoactive Drugs) $17.95. LC 87-29501. ISBN 0-877-54766-1.

This book explains the effects of psychoactive drugs on the senses. Experiences are described such as distorted self-image, paranoia, damage to the sensory organs, and confusion of reality and illusion. Chapter titles include "Keeping in Touch with the World," "Fooling the Senses," "Marijuana," "LSD and Other Hallucinogens," "Opiates: Creating the Illusion of Well-Being," "PCP: A Giant Step Backward," and "Cocaine and Inhalants." The appendix includes a list of state agencies for the prevention and treatment of drug abuse and a glossary of 40 terms.

NF

Check, William A. **Drugs of the Future.** New York: Chelsea House, 1987. 116p. illus. (The Encyclopedia of Psychoactive Drugs) $17.95. LC 87-732. ISBN 1-555-46208-1.

The increasing role of chemical substances in treating mental illness is examined. The discussion of chemicals and their effect on body functions includes reproduction and growth and provides a theory on the expanding role synthetic drugs will have in the future. Chapter titles include "The Brain's Chemical Factory," "Mental Illness: A Need for Better Drugs," "Antianxiety Drugs of the Future," "Treatment of Depression: A Continuing Success Story," "The Body's Own Morphine," "Treasure Chest of Chemicals," and "Feeling Good Can Keep You Well." The appendix includes a list of state agencies for the prevention and treatment of drug abuse and a glossary of 50 terms.

FIC

Childress, Alice. **A Hero Ain't Nothin' But a Sandwich.** New York: Coward McCann and Geoghegan, 1973. 126p. $8.95. LC 73-82035. ISBN 698-20278-3. Avon (Flare), 1982. 128p. $2.50. ISBN 0-380-00132-2. (GR 7-up)

The setting for this novel is an urban black ghetto. Benjie, an engaging thirteen-year-old, is on his way to being hooked on heroin. Several people, however, care and are available to help. The story is touching and well told with occasional flashes of humor, although the harsh realities of ghetto life and poverty are seen through the principal characters who tell their stories in the first person. The book offers no easy solutions, but it ends satisfactorily because Benjie seems to be able to cope with life, and people who matter stand by him. This is a very good book, although the black dialect used may be difficult for some readers to understand.

NF

Chiles, John. **Teenage Depression and Suicide.** New York: Chelsea House, 1986. 102p. illus. (The Encyclopedia of Psychoactive Drugs) $17.95. LC 86-976. ISBN 0-877-54771-8.

The role drugs play in the emotions of teenagers is set in the context of the causes of teenage depression and suicide. Chapter titles include "The Many Faces of Suicidal Behavior," "Adolescent Suicide," "Families and Suicide," "Drugs and Suicide," "Assessing Suicidal Behavior," and "Helping Someone Who Has Overdosed." The appendix includes a list of state agencies for the prevention and treatment of drug abuse and a glossary with 36 terms.

NF

Chomet, Julian. **Cocaine and Crack.** New York: Watts, 1987. 64p. (Understanding Drugs) $11.90. LC 87-50600. ISBN 0-531-10435-4.

One of a series of books discussing the motivation for taking drugs, in this case cocaine and crack. Factual, well-organized information presents the origin, nature, and effects of cocaine and its highly addictive and dangerous new form, crack. The physical and psychological effects, the possibility of addiction, and the possibility for cure are presented as well as efforts to halt their abuse. Includes sources of help, addresses, hotlines, and other information.

Reviewed in *Booklist*, January 1, 1988, and *School Library Journal*, February 1988.

NF
Claypool, Jane. **Alcohol and You.** New York: Watts, 1988. 128p. $12.95. LC 88-10258. ISBN 0-531-10566-0. (GR 8-12)

The causes and effects of teenage drinking are given as well as information on getting help to overcome the habit. The book provides teenagers with an informed choice and discusses how this informed choice should affect their decision about drinking.

Reviewed in *Wilson Library Bulletin*, May 1989.

VHS
Cocaine & the Student Athlete. Northbrook, IL: Film Ideas, 1986. 29 min. video. $185.00.

Through interviews with professional athletes, a sports psychologist, an adolescent rehabilitation counselor, a narcotics detective, and doctors, student athletes can learn why athletes turn to drugs. Short- and long-term effects are discussed. Topics covered include why cocaine is getting attention, why athletes use cocaine, the attitudes of cocaine users, and warning signs that are symptoms of addiction. A former college football player indicted on cocaine charges explains the consequences of his cocaine use.

FLM/VHS
Cocaine: Beyond the Looking Glass. New York: Phoenix Films, 1987. 25 min. film, $495.00; video, $300.00.

Recovering addicts tell their stories emphasizing that cocaine is addictive. Viewers are introduced to the Narcotics Anonymous program.

NF
Coffey, Wayne. **Straight Talk About Drinking: Teenagers Speak Out About Alcohol.** New York: NAL (New American Library) Plume, 1988. 164p. appendix. $7.95 pa. LC 87-32446. ISBN 0452-26061-2. (GR 9-12)

This author compares his experiences as the son of an alcoholic mother with those of fifty other teenagers, some of whom are alcoholics themselves. He also includes information from a medical director of the alcohol and drug treatment center at the University of Connecticut, Dr. James O'Brien, in explaining the physiological and psychological effects of alcohol on users. Particular attention is paid to the effects of drinking and driving and to coping with an alcoholic at home.

Reviewed in *Booklist*, September 15, 1988.

NF
Cohen, Daniel, and Susan Cohen. **A Six-Pack and a Fake I.D.: Teens Look at the Drinking Question.** New York: M. Evans, 1986. 156p. bibliog. $11.95. LC 85-25337. ISBN 0-87131-459-2.

The role of drinking in our society is presented beginning with a scenario of getting a fake I.D. Beginning to drink and suggestions for how to handle hangovers follow. The various reasons people drink are given as well as the physiological effects of alcoholic beverages. Popular misconceptions about alcohol are discussed as well as the differences between drunkenness and alcoholism. Through descriptions of individuals and their reaction to alcohol, the book strives to give all aspects of the issue of alcohol consumption so that teenagers can make an informed decision to drink or not to drink. "Practical Stuff" includes addresses for Students Against Driving Drunk (SADD), Mothers Against Drunk Driving (MADD), Remove Intoxicated Drivers (RID), Alliance Against Intoxicated Motorists (AAIM), and Alcoholics Anonymous (AA).

NF

Cohen, Miriam. **Marijuana: Its Effects on Mind and Body.** New York: Chelsea House, 1985. 126p. illus. (The Encyclopedia of Psychoactive Drugs) $17.95. LC 84-29261. ISBN 0-877-54754-8.

An exploration of the scientific, social, and personal aspects of marijuana. The book traces the history, cultural impact, physiological and psychological effects, dangers, and legal status of marijuana. For the debate team, this book iterates the pros and cons of the legalization issue. Chapter titles include "The Hows and Whys of 'Getting High'," "What Is Marijuana?," "The History of Marijuana," "How Many People Use Marijuana," "Marijuana and Your Health," "The Treatment of Marijuana Abuse," "Marijuana and the Law," and "Marijuana's Future." The appendix covers government and voluntary agencies, state and federal marijuana laws, marijuana eradication statistics, state agencies for the prevention and treatment of drug abuse, and a chronology of marijuana in the U.S.

NF

Cohen, Sidney, ed. **Drug Abuse and Alcoholism: Current Critical Issues.** New York: Haworth Press, 1981. 62p. bibliog. (Collected Essay Series.) $6.95 pa. LC 79-25648. ISBN 0-917724-10-0.

Some of the material included in this collection of essays has been reprinted from other sources. It is a scholarly but clearly presented analysis of the current scene in substance abuse. The editor points out that change marks this scene. New therapies arise—and will fall; new prevention techniques are developed; and new problems arise, although the old ones remain unsolved.

Seven reviews written by various experts on important facets of substance abuse are included. Titles are "Street Drugs 1977: Changing Patterns of Recreational Use," "Marijuana—Our Next Step," "The Psychosocial Characteristics of Alcoholic Women," "The Identification and Management of Alcoholic and Depressive Problems," "Heroin Maintenance: The Second Time Around," "Hypnotic Drug Therapy," and "Forensic Psychopharmacology: The Drug Abuse Expert in Court." Also included is a glossary of key terms.

Although the publication is most suitable perhaps for the advanced reader, it is recommended for all because it discusses drug problems that should be understood and dealt with. It is pointed out that the social, economic, health, and familial costs of substance abuse are enormous.

NF

Cohen, Sidney. **The Drug Dilemma.** 2d ed. New York: McGraw-Hill, 1976. 103p. bibliog. $24.95; $17.95 pa. LC 75-12901. ISBN 0-07-011587-7; 0-07-01588-5 pa.

The first edition of this short book was published in 1969. This second edition is almost a new work because the drug scene has changed so much. Cohen sees the new phase as more stable, but warns that we have not resolved the drug problem. The book was written for those who teach or counsel young people, but students and parents should also find it quite valuable. Cohen is a physician whose chief research interest is psychopharmacology, but his book is easy to read as well as authentic, astute, and interesting.

The book discusses the drug scene, showing trends and developments and outlining the effects, side effects, methods of treatment, and ways of preventing drug abuse. Chapter headings are "Those Who Will Not Learn from History....," "Some Definitions," "The Psychedelics ... LSD and Others," "The Psychedelics ... Marihuana," "Amphetamines, Cocaine, and Other Stimulants," "The Narcotics," "The Sedatives and Tranquilizers," "The Volatile Solvents and Other Anesthetics," "Alcohol, a Dangerous Drug," "Deliriant, Old and New," "The 'Head'," and "The Drug Dilemmas." In addition, there is a drug glossary, a table summarizing drug effects, and a list of additional readings.

FIC

Cole, Barbara. **Alex the Great.** New York: Rosen, 1989. 73p. (Flipside Fiction Series) $12.95. LC 88-37104. ISBN 0-8239-0941-7. (GR 8-12)

Concepts of loyalty and responsibility are tested when a high school tennis star, Deonna, must decide what to do about her best friend. Alex Starky is a drug addict and dealer who has been placed in a drug rehabilitation program. After causing a friend's death, Alex tried to commit suicide. This book is designed so that half the book features one viewpoint, and the other half presents the opposing perception. Most readers will find this novel much less interesting than *A Hero Ain't Nothin' But a Sandwich*.

Reviewed in *School Library Journal*, June 1989.

NF

Cox, W. Miles. **The Addictive Personality.** New York: Chelsea House, 1986. 96p. illus. (The Encyclopedia of Psychoactive Drugs) $17.95. LC 86-988. ISBN 0-877-54773-4.

Personality and addictive behavior are traced from the historical view of the ancient Greeks through Carl Jung and Sigmund Freud. Freud's theory that children frustrated at the oral stage of development will be more likely to smoke, drink, and overeat is explained. Cox stresses that the simplistic concept of an "addictive personality" cannot explain a complex phenomenon. Methods of studying addiction are discussed. The volume has many excellent illustrations, including one picture of television viewers with the caption, "Television viewing is a common, often intense psychological addiction. One study found that regular TV watchers, when deprived of their sets, felt a sense of loss comparable to that caused by a death in the family." While alcoholism is featured, other forms of addiction are covered. The appendix includes a list of state agencies for the prevention and treatment of drug abuse, a bibliography for further reading, and a glossary of 41 terms including "Oedipus complex" and "thematic apperception test." An attempt is made to determine whether there are characteristic traits before as well as after addiction.

FLM/VHS

Crack. New York: Phoenix Films, 1987. 25 min. film, $495.00; video, $300.00.

First discovered in the Bronx of New York City, crack can now be found all over the United States. It is one of the most insidious and powerful drugs ever, and is widely used at this time. Addicts and former addicts are shown in real-life situations and during group therapy sessions.

FLM/VHS

Cruel Spirits: Alcohol and Violence. Produced by: Dystar Television. Deerfield, IL: Coronet/MTI, 1989. film, $595.00; video, $495.00. (GR 9-12)

The effects of alcohol on automobile deaths and drowning, and on murders, rapes, and other crimes are described. Victims described include unborn infants of alcoholic mothers and abused children. Interviews a variety of persons who are well aware of the consequences of alcohol and violence—emergency room personnel, police, and recovered alcoholics—and who provide first-hand evidence to support the statistics presented. The viewer is asked to consider why this substance is so easy to abuse in our society, pointing out the environment of advertisements, social occasions, parties, and bars that surround the drinker.

Reviewed in *School Library Journal*, September 1989.

NF

Daley, Dennis C. **Surviving Addiction: A Guide for Alcoholics, Drug Addicts, and Their Families.** New York: Gardner Press, Inc., 1988. 251p. index. $19.95. LC 87-21106. ISBN 0-89876-146-8.

Through case studies, basic information is presented on addiction, e.g., how users become addicted, effects, rehabilitation, relapse, and the role of family. The volume is divided into four parts: "Introduction to Addiction," "The Alcoholic and Drug Addict," "The Family," and "Conclusions." Within these parts topics covered include "Alcohol and Drug Addiction: Diseases that Affect Everyone," "How People Become Addicted and Stay That Way," "The Effects of Addiction on the Alcoholic or Drug-Addicted Person," "Getting Well: The Recovery Journey," "Relapse Prevention: Reserving a Seat on the Recovery Wagon," "Where to Get Help: Programs for Alcoholics and Drug Addicts," "Getting the Alcoholic or Drug Addict to Accept Help," "What Addiction Really Does to the Family," "Living on a Roller Coaster: Being Married to an Alcoholic or Drug Addict," "Innocent Victims: The Children," "Recovery of the Family," "Family Relapse Prevention," and "Where the Family Can Get Help." The appendix includes a bibliography with 114 entries coded by audience, aimed at helping to understand addiction and recovery, effects on family, effects on young children, effects on adult children, and the twelve steps of Alcoholics Anonymous, plus a list of publishers of information on addiction and recovery.

FS/FLM

Danger Ahead. Shawnee Mission, KA: Marshfilm, 1988. 4 filmstrips with 4 cassettes or video. 13 min. ea. Teacher's guides. $37.50 ea. (GR 8-12)

Titles include "Danger Ahead: Drugs," "Danger Ahead: Alcohol," "Danger Ahead: Tobacco," and "Your Health Responsibilities." The first three follow a similar format with a narrator presenting a case of a teenager beginning to abuse a substance. A second narrator explains the physiological and psychological dangers. The filmstrips end with discussion questions. The last filmstrip suggests that, although teens have decided to use drugs, tobacco, and alcohol, they should not try to get their peers to join them.

Reviewed in *School Library Journal*, June 1989.

NF

Dardis, Tom. **The Thirsty Muse: Alcohol and the American Writer.** New York: Houghton, 1989. 292p. $18.95. LC 88-29394. ISBN 0-89919-376-5.

This biography of four great American writers shows how alcoholism stopped the great talents of Faulkner, Hemingway, and Fitzgerald. The fourth, O'Neill, was able to give up drinking and write and produce his most successful plays.

Reviewed in *School Library Journal*, July 1989.

NF

Debner, Claudia Bialke, ed. **Chemical Dependency: Opposing Viewpoints.** St. Paul, MN: Greenhaven Press, 1985. 241p. illus. bibliog. index. $11.95; $6.95 pa. LC 85-16404. ISBN 0-899-08376-5; 0-89908-351-X pa.

One of the more balanced works in the field, this uses the drug abuse laws to present opposing viewpoints about both causes and treatment of alcohol, tobacco, and other drug addictions. Some of the viewpoints are extremely unconventional: national drinking age should be lowered, cocaine use is sensationalized. Pros and cons are given for abstinence. The causes and treatment of drug abuse include the seriousness and harmfulness of alcohol and tobacco. Ads for alcohol are discussed as well as the legalization of marijuana and the effects of secondhand smoke. Dramatic personal accounts and clever use of editorial cartoons make for absorbing reading. Prior to each essay, the reader is reminded of the issues to keep in mind. Critical thinking skill activities are stressed. For the researcher looking for additional information, chapter bibliographies and the general book bibliography are excellent. The book also includes a list of organizations to contact.

NF

Deutsch, Charles. **Broken Bottles, Broken Dreams: Understanding and Helping the Children of Alcoholics.** New York: Teacher's College Press, 1982. 213p. $17.95; $13.95 pa. LC 81-5729. ISBN 0-8077-366-8; 0-8077-0266-3-X pa.

The author of this book has been an educational specialist in the Cambridge and Somerville (Massachusetts) Program of Alcoholism Rehabilitation (CASPAR). CASPAR was formulated in the early seventies as a program for teachers. Deutsch worked with a youthful group of problem drinkers composed primarily of children from alcoholic families. In this book he shares his observations, experiences, and insights into helping these unfortunate youths. Readers are invited to see into the hearts of the affected children with their characteristic denial, secrecy, and shame, and to be aware of the implications these traits have in alienating the victim for an entire lifetime. It is evident that without educational intervention, alcoholism will continue to snowball into succeeding generations. Children of alcoholics are 50 percent more likely to become alcoholics than is the general population, and 60 percent more likely to marry alcoholics.

Deutsch's plan is to mobilize youth professionals who are already engaged in working with children, including teachers, guidance counselors, school nurses, social workers, probation officers, and scoutmasters. This book is addressed to these groups, although alcoholism professionals could gain from reading the work also. Strategies for helping are presented. One chapter focuses on Al-Anon and Alateen. Two useful appendixes are included, one on signs and symptoms of alcoholism including indications useful in recognizing children of alcoholics. The other is a list of appropriate materials to be used with children.

This book does not describe a cure-all or provide deep insights into all the problems of the alcoholic family. It does, however, show how to begin and is a valuable addition to the literature on alcohol education for a group of vulnerable children.

FIC

DeVault, Christine. **Christy's Chance.** Santa Cruz, CA: Network Publications, 1987. 72p. $3.95. LC 87-018542. ISBN 0-94181-33-8.

The reader tries to help Christy make decisions about using marijuana and shares with her the consequences of each decision.

FIC

DeVault, Christine, and Bryan Strong. **Serena's Secret.** Santa Cruz, CA: Network Publications, 1987. 80p. $3.95 pa. LC 87-18541. ISBN 0-941816-32-X. (GR 7-9)

"It's your choice," in this "Plot Your Own Stories" fiction volume. Readers are given the opportunity to help Serena make decisions about alcohol. The consequences of each decision are related, and readers can return to choose the alternate action and trace that outcome.

Reviewed in *Book Report*, May-June 1988.

VHS

Different Like Me. Minneapolis, MN: The Johnson Institute, 1989. 30 min. video. $525.00.

This film is designed to help educators, counselors, and others identify and aid teenage children of alcoholic parents. Through the story of Jason, the child of an alcoholic parent, other children can learn that they can accept help, that they are not different from others, and that they need not feel alone. See also the companion book by Evelyn Leite, *Different Like Me: A Book for Teens Who Worry About Their Parents' Use of Alcohol/Drugs.*

NF

Dolan, Edward F. **Drugs in Sports.** New York: Watts, 1986. 122p. illus. LC 85-29521. ISBN 0-531-10157-6. (GR 7-10)

Are the citizens of the United States overemphasizing winning at any cost? "The desire for that winning edge which will help make you a champion is one of the main forces behind today's drug problem in sports." Drug use is described from ancient times through the present, with stories of the Kaffir tribesmen of South Africa, Tom Hicks in the 1904 Olympics, and others. Drug abuse by professional athletes continues to be publicized to a wide audience and discussed in news commentaries, editorials, and church sermons as well as classrooms. This book presents an overview of drug abuse in both amateur and professional sports and includes those drugs believed to be helpful in body building and improving athletic performance, such as anabolic steroids, amphetamines, brake drugs, cocaine, and marijuana. Recent cases involving sports stars and drug abuse are related as they affect the sports organizations to which the athletes belong and what the sports world has done to cope with drug abuse.

Reviewed in *School Library Journal*, March 1987.

NF

Dolan, Edward F. **International Drug Traffic.** New York: Watts, 1985. 112p. $11.90. LC 84-23440. ISBN 0-531k-04937-X. (GR 7-12)

This volume describes the traffic in cocaine, heroin, and marijuana, where the drugs originate, how they are processed, how they are smuggled into countries, and how they are distributed to users throughout the world. The effects of the drugs on users are presented as well as the methods used by governments who are working together to end the international drug trade. Chapters include "The Deadly Traffic," "Cocaine—The Drug of the 1980s," "Cocaine—Out from South America," "Cocaine—The American Traffic," "The Heroin Menace," "The Heroin Trade," "Marijuana—Highs for the World," "The Marijuana Traffic," and "Fighting the International Traffic." The bibliography "For Further Reading" includes citations to six books and twenty-three articles.

Reviewed in *Booklist*, May 15, 1985.

NF

Donahoe, Tom, and Neil Johnson. **Foul Play: Drug Abuse in Sports.** New York: Basil Blackwell, 1986. 189p. illus. glossary. indices. $16.95. LC 85-30624. ISBN 0-631-14844. (GR 9-12)

An overview of drug use among athletes both male and female. Stimulants, anabolic steroids, anxiolytics, and analgesics are discussed. Emphasis is placed on sports internationally and there is less information directed to sports in the United States.

Reviewed in *Science Books and Films*, January/February 1987.

FIC

Donlan, Joan. **I Never Saw the Sun Rise.** Minneapolis, MN: CompCare Publications, 1977. 199p. illus. $7.95 pa. LC 77-87738. ISBN 0-89638-007-6.

This book is a teenager's diary covering a year and a half. During that time the writer became addicted to alcohol and drugs and went through treatment to become well again. It is a sensitive, very private account by a talented writer. Line drawings and poems by the author have been included. Some insights into why teenagers use drugs can possibly be gained from the account, and it should interest parents, teachers, counselors, ministers, law enforcement officers, and physicians, as well as young people.

NF

Douglas, Mary, ed. **Constructive Drinking: Perspectives on Drink from Anthropology.** New York: Cambridge University Press, 1987. 304p. $42.50. LC 86-33388. ISBN 0-52133-504-3.

Sponsored by the International Commission on Anthropology of Food, this collection of essays covers the social and celebratory uses of drink. The approach is an anthropological one, and for a university audience.

FIC

Dow, Miriam, and Jennifer Regan, eds. **The Invisible Enemy: Alcoholism & the Modern Short Story.** St. Paul, MN: Graywolf Press, 1989. 237p. $9.50 pa. LC 89-31690. ISBN 1-55597-118-0. (GR 10-12)

This anthology includes sixteen short stories written by American authors. Each story covers one phase of alcoholism and its effect on the family as well as the alcoholic. Brief biographical notes of each of the sixteen authors are given.

Reviewed in *Booklist*, November-December 1989.

FLM/VHS

Dream on Deadly Wings. New York: Phoenix Films, 1982. 6 min. film, $155.00; video, $115.00.

Animation is used to show the psychological and physiological effects of drug use on the drug user. The film points out that continual use of any addictive or mind-altering substance will lead to both mental and physical destruction.

FLM/VHS

Drinking Driver: What Could You Do? 2d ed. Deerfield, IL: Coronet Film and Video, 1988. 14 min. film, $400.00; video, $250.00. (GR 8-up)

Using three cases, the problem of drinking and driving is posed for discussion. Teens question the ability of a driver to drive after drinking at a pregame party and a rock concert. The third situation is a teen who is asked to ride with another team member's intoxicated parent. Judgment after drinking, altered self-judgment, and the absorption rate of alcohol are discussed as related to driving.

Reviewed in *Booklist*, August 1989.

VHS

Drugs: How They Affect Body Chemistry. Director: Bill Call for Gary Lopez Productions. Pleasantville, NY: Human Relations Media, 1988. 30 min. video. guide. $159.00. (GR 8-12)

Drug substances that "enhance, mimic, or block the normal chemical action of the body" are illustrated with animated graphics and models of the human body. The effects of depressants and stimulants on neurons and the physiological basis of tolerance and addiction are explored.

Reviewed in *Booklist*, June 15, 1989.

VHS

Drugs, Your Friends and You: Handling Peer Pressure. Pleasantville, NY: Sunburst Communications, 1988. 24 min. video. $159.00. Teacher's Guide. (GR 5-9)

Teenagers are shown dealing with the peer pressure related to drugs and alcohol. In each segment, one teenager feels uncomfortable and the group discusses the situation. The segments provide an opportunity for open-ended discussion question so that the tape can be stopped and the audience can react. Assertive techniques are offered by the narrative.

Reviewed in *School Library Journal*, July 1989.

NF
Dupont, Robert L. **Stopping Alcohol and Other Drug Use Before It Starts: The Future of Prevention.** Rockville, MD: U.S. Department of Health and Human Services, Public Health Services, 1989. OSAP Prevention Monograph 1. 99p. free.

A publication sponsored by the Office of Substance Abuse Prevention and the Institute for Behavior and Health, Inc., this prevention monograph is first in a series that will make available the latest information on promising new approaches to prevention. Contents include defining alcohol and drug use, the epidemic of alcohol and other drug use, knowledge about prevention of alcohol and other drug use, identification of youths at high risk, reduction of risk of alcohol and other drug use, and proposed next steps. Appendix A contains a checklist of genetic risk and motivational factors, temperament risk factors, environmental risk and protective factors, and community risk and protective factors. Appendix B contains a classification of risk items. A risk check for parents to assess their children is given in Appendix C.

NF
Edelson, Edward. **Drugs and the Brain.** New York: Chelsea House, 1987. 109p. illus. (The Encyclopedia of Psychoactive Drugs) $17.95. LC 86-31764. ISBN 1-555-46209-X.

The effects on the brain of both beneficial and potentially damaging psychoactive drugs are discussed. Chapter titles include "How the Brain Works," "Opiates and the Brain," "Alcohol and the Brain," "Barbiturates, Tranquilizers, and Alcohol," "Stimulants: Cocaine and the Amphetamines," "Accidents, Good and Bad," and "Psychedelic Drugs." The appendix includes a list of state agencies for the prevention and treatment of drug abuse and a glossary of 38 terms.

NF
Edwards, Gabrielle. **Coping With Drug Abuse.** Rev. ed. New York: Rosen Publications, 1988. 136p. bibliog. index. (Personal Adjustment Series) $12.95. LC 83-3341. ISBN 0-8239-0769-4.

The author of this volume is an assistant principal at Franklin D. Roosevelt High School in Brooklyn. She details the history, myths, and perils of marijuana, hallucinogens, cocaine, heroin, tobacco, and others. Chapter titles include "Medicines Versus Drugs," "Marijuana and Other Hallucinogens," "The Amphetamines, a Family of Stimulants," "The Barbiturates, a Family of Sedatives," "Heroin, the Hard Narcotic," "Cocaine, the Fantasy Maker," "Sniffing Volatile Substances," "Alcohol, the Legal Intoxicant," "Tobacco, the Legal Carcinogen," "Caffeine: The Quiet 'Picker-Upper'," and "Toward Coping with Drug Abuse." There is some unevenness in the presentations of drugs and the information does not follow a regular format. For instance, in the chapter on amphetamines, names are given with the trade names, slang names, and medical uses. In the chapter on barbiturates, rules for administering are given and a case study followed by discussion questions. The chapter on cocaine begins with a discussion of the source while the chapter on sniffing volatile substances describes "Who are sniffers."

The glossary has eighty-three terms with very brief definitions including addictive (causing tissue tolerance); physical dependency; craving; and cancer (abnormal growth of cells). The bibliography includes twenty-five citations to books, the most recent published in 1986 and the oldest in 1966.

VHS

Enabling: Masking Reality. Minneapolis, MN: The Johnson Institute, 1989. 22 min. video. $445.00.

Narrated by Hugh Downs, this is the second in a series including *Back to Reality* and *Intervention: Facing Reality*. The video describes how attempts to be helpful may enable addicts for a time to escape the consequences of their addiction, allowing the addiction to become stronger. Real-life scenes show how friends, family members, and co-workers become a part of the unreal world of one addict. This video won the Golden Eagle Award of the CINE International Film Festival.

NF

Engel, Joel. **Addicted: In Their Own Words: Kids Talking About Drugs as Told to Joel Engel**. New York: TOR, 1989. 174p. $15.95; $3.95 pa. ISBN 0-312-93145-X; 0-812-59446-7 pa.

As stated in the introduction, these are stories from recorded interviews of ten adolescents 15 to 21 from all over the U.S., from all economic, racial, and religious backgrounds, who were in a rehabilitation center in southern California. The reader is taken through situations where parents were divorced, were unaware of the abuse until a crisis occurred, and where peer pressure was too great to withstand. Each story is different, yet alike, most were younger than 13 when they began substance abuse and early experimentation was with alcohol and marijuana. The picture painted is not pleasant. One addict recalls going into a dangerous neighborhood to get drugs and having his car stolen by a group that then tried to run over him with it.

Reviewed in *School Library Journal*, April 1990.

NF

Fairchild, Daniel, Thomas N. Fairchild, David Starr, and Ed Woolums. **Everything You Always Wanted to Know About Drinking Problems,** And Then a Few Things You Didn't Want to Know**. Miami FL: Health Communications, Inc., 1978. 119p. illus. $6.50 pa. ISBN 0-932194-04-4.

This excellent book is able to convey an important message in a few words. It is composed almost entirely of cartoons with short captions. The introduction succinctly points out that, although alcoholism has in the recent past been considered by many to be a disease, many diseases are stigmatized by the public. Classifying an alcohol problem as a disease does not necessarily eliminate any stigma. The basic message of the work is that an alcohol problem, although distasteful and no fun, is nothing more or less than a problem. It is all right to have problems and all right to ask for assistance.

There are six chapters: "Alcohol Affects Us All," "Who Has Alcohol Problems?," "Symptoms of an Alcohol Problem," "Why People Have Alcohol Problems," "What Can They Do?," and "What to Do in a Pinch." An appendix lists alcoholism program contacts by state.

In each chapter the cartoons and captions deliver a short, to-the-point, understandable message. The material is quite clever, even humorous, and will not offend. For example, in the chapter on "Symptoms of an Alcohol Problem," a caption asks, "Do you always have a reason to drink? ... such as, you're depressed, or you need to calm your nerves, or you've had an argument, it's Tuesday and so on." The person in the cartoon is sitting at the bar saying, "Drinks are on me. It's Groundhog Day!"

The book covers our culture's drinking problem, the statistics, the magnitude and scope of the problem, who is affected, how to measure the seriousness of the problem, and the reasons—personal, social, etc.—for it. Several treatment methods are described in the cartoons in chapter 5. Chapter 6 is a brief general message to alcoholics telling them the pain is their own responsibility, their own problem to solve. This is an exceptionally fine book, which treats a complex problem in a simple, sensible, and sensitive manner.

FLM/VHS
Family Matters. New York: Phoenix Films, 1987. 25 min. film, $495.00; video, $300.00.

A documentary about families learning to live with alcoholism, drug abuse, and eating disorders. The families are not unique, and most viewers could place themselves in the scenario. Viewers meet persons in the film who can help, and they are encouraged to survive whether or not the addict recovers.

FLM/VHS
The Feminine Mistake: The Next Generation. Produced by Shari Cookson and Kevin Jon Henry. Santa Monica, CA: Pyramid Film and Video, 1989. 32 min. film, $495.00; video, $295.00. (GR 6-adult)

This film presents the smoker from female teenager to the senior citizen. Medical tests are used to explain the health problems caused by smoking, including the testimony of a woman who lost her voice box because of her addiction.

Reviewed in *Booklist*, January 1, 1990.

FLM/VHS
The Final Score. Produced by Canvas Productions. Los Angeles: Churchill Films, 1989. 23 min. 30 sec. film, $455.00; video, $340.00. (GR 7-12)

The story of Alex, captain of his hockey team, who loses it all when he is arrested for drunk driving. Alex borrows his brother's car to go to a party, becomes drunk, and while driving home hits a girl without remembering it. At the end the film shows Alex entering the courtroom. His parents have refused to accompany him, his girlfriend can no longer see him, and he has lost his place on the hockey team. The hockey coach confronts the team with their responsibility for letting a friend drive while drunk.

Reviewed in *School Library Journal*, October 1989.

NF
Fishman, Ross. **Alcohol and Alcoholism.** New York: Chelsea House, 1986. 118p. illus. (The Encyclopedia of Psychoactive Drugs) $17.95. LC 85-32572. ISBN 0-877-54762-9.

This book begins with a history of alcohol use and the concept of alcohol as a "beneficial gift of God." In colonial America, alcohol was considered a medicinal healer. From temperance and prohibition to the present, attitudes have changed. The creation of Alcoholics Anonymous (AA) and Mothers Against Drunk Drivers (MADD) are two results of the concept that alcoholism should be controlled. Properties and effects of alcohol are described, and use, abuse, prevention, intervention, and treatments are given. The final chapter discusses "What You Can Do." Prevention is explained as related to adolescents, young children, the elderly, the multi-disabled, homosexuals, multiple substance abusers, the indigent, and ex-offenders, through education, legislation, drinking-age laws, taxes, warning labels, advertising, and intervention programs. The appendix includes state agency addresses for the prevention and treatment of drug abuse, six items in a bibliography, and a thirty-four-term glossary.

NF

FitzGerald, Kathleen W. **Alcoholism: The Inside Story.** New York: Doubleday, 1988. 239p. glossary. bibliog. $17.95. LC 87-9114. ISBN 0-385-19933-3.

This volume will be especially helpful for readers interested in the debate of whether alcoholism is a disease. The medical profession has considered it a disease for more than twenty-five years; yet, this is not universally accepted. The author, an alcoholic, presents research to corroborate the genetic propensity for alcoholism and the existence of a biochemical component making certain people more susceptible than others.

Reviewed in *Booklist*, July 1988.

NF

Forrest, Gary G. **How to Cope with a Teenage Drinker: New Alternatives and Hope for Parents and Families.** New York: Atheneum, 1983. 174p. $10.95. LC 82-73023. ISBN 0-689-11346-3.

Addressed primarily to parents of the teenage boy and girl who abuses alcohol, this book offers guidelines to help both the teenager and the parent. No miracle cures are offered, but the book shows there is hope.

Forrest begins by saying that alcoholism affects the whole family. Family members often develop psychosomatic stress symptoms and feel depressed, guilty, anxious, and angry. The core of the message of the book is that while family members cannot control or directly change the drinker, they can help themselves and indirectly effect healthy changes on the part of the teenage drinker.

Chapter headings are: "Helping the Teenage Drinker by Helping Yourself," "Teenage Drinking Patterns," "Why Teenagers Drink," "How to Recognize a Teenage Alcohol Abuser," "Personality Features of the Teenage Alcohol Abuser," "Family 'Rules' and Roles that Promote Alcohol Abuse," "Family 'Rules' and Roles that Thwart Alcohol Abuse," "Help for the Teenage Drinker: Treatment Alternatives," "A Prescription for Change for the Parents and Families of Teenage Drinkers," and "Recovery and Beyond."

The author concludes by saying that every teenage alcoholic does not recover. Parents should realize that in such cases: (1) They are entitled to choose not to have the teenage drinker continue living in the home, (2) They (the parents) must be prepared to make this decision, and (3) They can survive without the teenage alcohol abuser; in a few cases, this may be the only way for the family to live.

FIC

Fosburgh, Liza. **Cruise Control.** New York: Bantam, 1988. 217p. $13.95. LC 88-10495. ISBN 0-553-0549-1-0. (GR 6-9)

In this fiction book, the sixteen-year-old hero, Gussie, becomes increasingly desperate in trying to cope with his mother's growing mental instability as a result of alcohol abuse and in trying to convince his "do it ourselves" father to seek outside aid.

Reviewed in *Publisher's Weekly*, August 26, 1988.

NF

Foster, Carol D., Nancy R. Jacobs, and Mark A. Siegel, eds. **Illegal Drugs and Alcohol: America's Anguish.** Wylie, TX: Information Plus, 1989. illus. charts. maps. (The Information Series on Current Topics) $19.95. ISBN 0936474947. (GR 9-12)

This paperback volume contains a wealth of statistics on such topics as "Seriousness of Drug-Related Neighborhood Crime" from The Gallup Poll and the Bureau of Justice, among other not-easily-found sources. Chapter titles include "Alcohol and Drugs—A Long and Varied History," "Alcohol—What It Is and What It Does," "Alcohol Consumption in the United States," "Alcohol Abuse and Alcoholism," "Drugs of Abuse—Uses and Effects," "Drug Use and Treatment," "Drugs, Alcohol, Smoking and Youth," "Drug Trafficking," "Drugs and Crime," "Fighting Drugs—Prevention and Treatment," "Drug Testing in the Workplace," "Intravenous Drug Abuse and AIDS," and "Tobacco Use and Its Consequences." Information given is up-to-date and brief, and would be of particular interest to students writing papers and needing further confirmation of less timely statistics found in other sources.

NF

Freeman, Sally. **Drugs and Civilization.** New York: Chelsea House, 1988. 112p. illus. (The Encyclopedia of Psychoactive Drugs) $17.95. LC 87-23273. ISBN 1-555-46222-7.

This book explores the history of drug use relating the role and effect of drugs on various societies from earliest times to the present. Chapter titles include "Drugs, Magic, and Religion," "Medicinal Uses of Drugs," "Drugs and Creativity," "Drugs, Trade, and Economics," and "Drugs, Recreation, and Rebellion." The appendix includes a list of state agencies for the prevention and treatment of drugs and a glossary with fifty-eight terms.

NF

Friedland, Bruce. **Emotions and Thoughts.** New York: Chelsea House, 1988. 127p. (The Encyclopedia of Psychoactive Drugs) $17.95. LC 88-9538. ISBN 1-555-46205-7.

The effects of drug use on normal emotions and the thinking process are presented. Chapter titles include "What Is Normal?," "Personality," "The Nature of Emotion," "Learning," "Emotion," "Memory," "Sensation and Perception," "Human Sexuality," and "Altered States of Consciousness." The appendix includes a glossary with forty-two terms.

NF

Furst, Peter E. **Mushrooms, Psychedelic Fungi.** New York: Chelsea House, 1986. 127p. illus. (The Encyclopedia of Psychoactive Drugs) $17.95. LC 85-17522. ISBN 0-877-54767-X.

One of nature's oldest and, perhaps, most misunderstood drugs is the psychedelic mushroom. This book discusses the uses and the hallucinogenic properties of this mushroom. Chapter titles include "The World of the Fungi,"

"Mushrooms of the Gods," "Amanita Muscasia, the Sacred Mushroom of Siberia," "Morphology and Ecology of the Fly Agaric," "Effects of Phallotoxins," "The Fly Agaric in the New World," "The Magic Mushrooms of Indian America," and "Psilocybe Use in the United States." The appendix includes a list of state agencies for the treatment and prevention of drug abuse and a glossary with fifty-nine terms.

NF

Gahagan, Dolly D., and Frederick G. Gahagan. **Switch Down and Quit: What the Cigarette Companies Don't Want You to Know About Smoking.** Berkeley, CA: Ten Speed Press, 1987. 128p. tables. $5.95 pa. LC 86-30161. ISBN 0-89815-204-6. (GR 9-12)

The authors, former smokers and formerly involved in the marketing of cigarettes, suggest ways to stop smoking. They also use their expertise in a chapter showing how advertisers work to keep their customers smoking and highlight the relationship between the tobacco industry, its marketing plan, and its profit-making motives. Their quit-smoking plan includes changing brands on a three-week cycle.

Reviewed in *Booklist*, December 15, 1987.

NF

Gilbert, Richard J. **Caffeine: The Most Popular Stimulant.** New York: Chelsea House, 1986. 154p. illus. (The Encyclopedia of Psychoactive Drugs) $17.95. LC 85-25970. ISBN 0-877-54756-4.

Caffeine found in coffee, tea, and soft drinks as well as many other foods and beverages is a popular, heavily used stimulant. This book explores the nature and both harmful and beneficial effects of this drug. Chapter titles include "The History of Tea and Coffee," "Sources of Caffeine," "Caffeine's Chemistry and Biochemistry," "How Caffeine Is Used," "Trade in Coffee and Tea," "Caffeine Consumption," "Caffeine in the Body," "Variation in Response to Caffeine," "Caffeine's Effect on the Brain, Behavior, Mood, and Sleep," "The Acute Effects of Caffeine," "Dependence on Caffeine," and "Effects of Chronic Use of Caffeine." The appendix includes a list of state agencies for the prevention and treatment of drug abuse and a glossary with seventy-seven terms.

NF

Gilbert, Sara D. **Get Help: Solving the Problems in Your Life.** New York: Morrow, 1989. 130p. $12.95; $7.95 pa. LC 88-32352. ISBN 0-688-08010-3; 0-688-08928-3. (GR 6-12)

For students who recognize they need help, this well-organized, basic guide provides addresses, telephone numbers, and ways to handle emergencies. In addition, information is given that will help the teenager approach the helping service. Some topics included are abuse, addiction, disabilities, eating disorders, education, scholarships available, legal matters, and mental health.

NF
Glowa, John R. **Inhalants: The Toxic Fumes.** New York: Chelsea House, 1986. 108p. illus. index. (The Encyclopedia of Psychoactive Drugs) $17.95. LC 85-32569. ISBN 0-877-54758-0.

When used as inhalants, volatile hydrocarbons such as paint thinners, glue, and cleaning fluid have become a rapidly growing form of drug abuse. This book investigates the use of toxic fumes as a drug. Chapters include "The History of Solvents," "The Chemistry and Pharmacology of Solvents," "Exposure to Solvents," "The Behavioral Effects of Inhalants," "The Health Effects of Solvent Abuse," "The Epidemiology of Solvent Abuse," and "Inhalants and the Law." The appendix provides addresses and telephone numbers for state agencies for the prevention and treatment of drug abuse, further reading, and a glossary of fifty-three terms. The book also includes information concerning the results of toxic fumes and substances involuntarily inhaled such as black lung disease and lead-based paint poisoning. One section addresses "Establishing Safe Solvent Levels."

NF
Godfrey, Martin. **Heroin.** New York: Watts, 1987. 64p. illus. (Understanding Drugs) $11.90. LC 87-50599. ISBN 0-531-10436-2.

One of a series of books discussing the motivation for taking drugs, in this case heroin. Its origin, nature, and effects are traced. The physiological and psychological effects, and the possibility of addiction, are described as well as efforts to halt its abuse and the possibility for cure.

Reviewed in *Booklist*, January 1, 1988, and *School Library Journal*, February 1988.

NF
Godfrey, Martin. **Marijuana.** New York: Watts, 1987. 64p. illus. (Understanding Drugs) $11.90. index. ISBN 0-531-10437-0.

This book presents a discussion of the psychological reasons people use marijuana and the physical effects of the drug. The plant is described along with its health risks and distribution sources. Sources for getting help are suggested. There are many excellent photographs, charts, and drawings that would appeal to junior high students. Quotes from users, highlighted in red, are interspersed throughout the text.

Reviewed in *Booklist*, January 1, 1988.

NF
Golden, Sandy. **Driving the Drunk off the Road: A Handbook for Action.** Washington, DC: Acropolis Books, 1983. 178p. $7.95. LC 83-8982. ISBN 0-87491-7440 pa. (GR 9 12)

This book offers specific steps to be taken at local, state, and national levels to change drunk driving policy. Teenagers can become activists and personal advocates to halt drunk drivers. The author presents statistics and case histories about the problem and gives information about organizing Students Against Drink Drivers (SADD). Strategies are outlined for projects, public relations activities, working with community lawmakers, and testing community systems for dealing with drunk drivers. Finally, draft wording and sample documents are proposed for drunk driving laws.

NF

Goodman, Paula, and Gabriel Koz. **Designer Drugs.** New York: Chelsea House, 1988. 116p. illus. (The Encyclopedia of Psychoactive Drugs) $17.95. LC 87-26835. ISBN 1-555-46207-3.

The first chapter, "What Are Designer Drugs?," says they are called that "because the jet-set uses them. They're glamorous drugs—like cocaine," and they "cost a lot, like designer jeans." Other chapters are "The Body's Own Drugs," "Three Major Designer Drugs," "Two Cautionary Tales from the Street," "The Special Status of Adolescents," "Fighting Back," and "Drug-Free Alternatives." The appendix includes a list of state agencies for the prevention and treatment of drug abuse, a six-item bibliography, and a glossary of thirty-six terms.

NF

Goodwin, Donald W. **Alcohol and the Writer.** Rev. ed. New York: Penguin Books, 1990. 136p. $12.95. (Personal Adjustment Series) LC 89-36512. ISBN 0-1401-2655-4.

The author, a psychiatrist, believes that alcoholism among American writers is rampant. Poe, Hemingway, Faulkner, Fitzgerald and Steinbeck are just a few of the writers profiled. While many other behavior disorders are obscured by alcoholism, Goodwin stands behind his thesis. He does state that most of his subjects cannot be labeled alcoholics.

NF

Goplerud, Eric N. **Breaking New Ground for Youth at Risk, Program Summaries.** Rockville, MD: U.S. Department of Health and Human Services, Public Health Services, 1990. OSAP Technical Reports No. 1. 137p. free

Prepared by the Office for Substance Abuse Prevention, this volume is the first in a series of technical reports designed to facilitate the transfer of prevention and intervention technology between and among researchers, administrators, policymakers, educators, and providers in the public and private sectors. Contents include numbers of U.S. youth at high risk, risk factors, protection factors, prevention theory, research related to high-risk youth, overviews of grants, and project summaries. An index of grants is given at the end of the book.

NF

Goulart, Frances Sheridan. **The Caffeine Book (A User's and Abuser's Guide).** New York: Dodd-Mead, 1984. 210p. LC 84-1602. ISBN 0-396-08371-4.

Chapter titles include "Caffeine—The Great American Addiction," "What You Need to Know About Coffee," "What You Need to Know About Decaffeinated Coffee," "What You Need to Know About Tea," "What You Need to Know About Soda Pop," "What You Need to Know About Chocolate," "What You Need to Know About Over-the-Counter Drugs," "What You Should Know About Caffeine-Related Illnesses," "Sizing Up the Problem: How Much Caffeine Is Too Much?," and "Alternatives." The volume also provides a caffeine-user's quiz, a ten-step program for kicking the caffeine habit, a ten-step caffeine-free maintenance plan, and a list of caffeine-free coffees, teas, colas, and cocoas to make and buy as well as twenty-five ways to consume less caffeine. The "Notes" section will lead students to a wide variety of additional sources in newspapers and magazines, but they are, because of the age of this book, very dated.

NF
Graeber, Laurel. **Are You Dying for a Drink? Teenagers and Alcohol Abuse.** New York: Messner, 1985. 160p. appendix. bibliog. index. (Teen Survival Library Series) $9.79. LC 85-8880. ISBN 0-671-50818-0. (GR 7-up)

The life of a teenager who drinks too much is described with suggestions about who is likely to become an alcoholic. Why teens drink is discussed and testimonials from teens who had drinking problems are given. The storytelling technique makes the nature of the problem very clear. The effects of alcohol on the body and the mind are presented, along with treatment for alcoholism. The book also covers drinking and driving and living with alcoholic parents. National organizations concerned with drug and alcohol abuse are listed. A bibliography, index, and appendix of resources are included.

Reviewed in *School Library Journal*, February 1986.

NF
Grauer, Neil A. **Drugs and the Law.** New York: Chelsea House, 1988. 120p. illus. (The Encyclopedia of Psychoactive Drugs) $17.95. LC 87-38230. ISBN 1-555-462308.

This volume discusses past problems and new procedures relating to the legal control of drug abuse. Chapters include "Prohibition—How Dry We Weren't," "Tobacco: Smoke Gets in Your Eyes," "Once Legal, Now Outlawed: The Evolution of Illicit-Drug Laws," "The Worldwide Battle Against Drugs," "You're Not in Kansas Anymore," "Drug Searching and Testing," and "Legalization? Probably Not." The appendix contains a list of state agencies for the prevention and treatment of drug abuse, a fourteen-item bibliography, and a glossary with forty-eight terms.

FIC
Green, Shep. **The Boy Who Drank Too Much.** New York: Viking Press, 1979. 160p. $11.50. LC 78-26370. ISBN 0-670-18381-4. (GR 7-up)

This book, aimed at the juvenile reader, is a fictional account of the life of a teenage alcoholic. The young victim's father is responsible for the death of the boy's mother, who died in a car crash because of the father's drinking. The father relieves his tensions by beating the boy and relives his past achievements by pushing his son to excel on the school hockey team. The son is isolated and lonely and takes to drink. His condition deteriorates until he begins to accept help. The author gives a realistic description of the results of alcohol abuse, but shows how victims can be helped.

FIC
Guy, Rosa. **The Ups and Downs of Carl Davis III.** New York: Delacorte, 1989. 113p. $13.95. LC 88-23693. ISBN 0-385-2792X-6.

Carl's parents send him from Brooklyn to rural South Carolina where he will live with his grandmother and avoid the drug scene. Written as a series of letters to his parents, this novel touches only briefly on substance abuse.

Reviewed in *School Library Journal*, June 1989.

NF

Gwynne, Peter. **Who Uses Drugs?** New York: Chelsea House, 1988. 110p. illus. index. (The Encyclopedia of Psychoactive Drugs) $17.95. LC 87-13259. ISBN 1-555-46223-5.

Different drugs are abused by various segments of the population. This book discusses the indigent, women, teenagers, celebrities, blue collar workers, and professionals who are drug users. Chapter titles include "Defining the Problem," "Drugs in the Workplace," "Public Safety at Risk," "The Big Stars" (including athletes in baseball, football, and basketball and entertainers), "Women and Drugs" (including the superwoman syndrome), "Young People Turning On, Tuning Out," "Down and Out in the Inner City," and "Signs of Hope." Appendixes include a list of state agencies for the prevention and treatment of drug abuse, a seven-item bibliography, and a twenty-five-term glossary.

NF

Hafen, Brent Q. **Alcohol.** 2d ed. St. Paul, MN: West Publishing Co., 1983. 290p. illus. bibliog. index. $22.25. LC 82-20270. ISBN 0-314-69652-0. (Revised edition of **Alcohol, the Crutch That Cripples**)

Although this work is intended primarily as a text for undergraduate college courses in the social and health sciences, it can be recommended to anyone interested in the problem of alcoholism. A good deal of the material has been taken word-for-word or summarized from publications of government agencies such as the National Institute of Mental Health and the National Institute on Alcohol Abuse and Alcoholism.

A rather wide range of topics involving drinking behavior and alcoholism is covered. Chapter headings are "Introduction: Alcohol and Its Use," "Effects of Alcoholic Beverages on the Body," "Alcohol-Related Problems," "Interaction of Alcohol and Other Drugs," "Problem Drinking and Alcoholism," "Social Problems and Excessive Drinking," "Treatment of Alcoholism," "Preventing Alcohol Problems and Alcoholism," "Laws, Regulations, and Drinking Patterns," and "Alcohol Emergencies."

The chapter on the effects of alcohol on the body is especially well done as it makes the subject clear to the layperson. The treatment chapter is also quite successful. It describes a number of therapeutic approaches, and the author speaks for the use of a combination of these, a plan usually considered the most effective.

As is stated in the preface, the book represents a gleaning from the research and writings of prominent experts in the field.

NF

Hales, Dianne R. **Case Histories.** New York: Chelsea House, 1987. 104p. illus. (The Encyclopedia of Psychoactive Drugs) $17.95. LC 87-526. ISBN 1-555-46217-0.

This book cites the case histories of ten men, women, and teens who never imagined they would become addicts or alcoholics. While written as anonymous stories, these tales tell of the live of celebrities, teens, and parents of teenagers from all ethnic backgrounds, races, religions, and political groups sharing the common problem of drug abuse. Chapters include "Jimmy: Under the Influence," "Jennifer: All in the Family," "David: 'It's Only Pot'," "Sherri: Fifteen Years of Addiction," "Nick: A Cokeaholics Tale," "Sandy: No Place to

Run," "Jeff: Life and Death on the Streets," "Marianne: Poor Little Fat Girl," and "Keith: A Junkie's Journey." The book also includes a picture essay, "Getting Help." The appendix includes a list of state agencies for the prevention and treatment of drug abuse, a six-item bibliography, and a glossary with thirty terms.

NF

Handbook on the Anti-Drug Abuse Act of 1986. Washington, D.C.: United States Government Printing Office, 1987. 131p. bibliog. $8.00 pa. LC 87-601477. ISBN 027-000-01269-8.

Prepared to assist federal prosecutors and investigators with this new law, the book may be of interest to others. There are fifteen subtitles to Title I of the act including Narcotics Penalties and Enforcement Act, Controlled Substances Import and Export Act, Penalties Enhancement Act, Drug Possession Penalty Act, Juvenile Drug Trafficking Act, Assets Forfeiture Amendments Act (including Money Laundering Forfeiture Amendments), Controlled Substances Technical Amendments, Controlled Substance Analog Enforcement Act, Continuing Drug Enterprise Act, Money Laundering Control Act, Armed Career Criminals, Narcotics Traffickers Deportation Act, Freedom of Information Act, Prohibition of the Interstate Sale and Transportation of Drug Paraphernalia, Manufacturing Operations, and Common Carrier Operation Under the Influence of Alcohol or Drugs. Title II is the International Narcotics Control Act. Subtitles for Title III include Customs Enforcement Act, Maritime Drug Law Enforcement, and Transportation Safety. Title XV is the National Forest System Drug Control Act. Appendixes include a shorthand chronology of drug-related bills enacted since 1970, a listing of the present status of criminal fines in drug cases, a discussion of Coast Guard enforcement of drug trafficking laws, and the outline of new money-laundering offenses.

VHS

Hard Facts About Drugs: Alcohol, Marijuana, Cocaine and Crack. Mount Kisco, NY: Guidance Associates, 1988. 22 min. video. $59.00. (GR 9-12)

The psychological and physiological effects of addiction are shown through the lives of four addicted teenagers from the same freshman class. One boy, Marty, is shown as a heavy drinker, and another, Kevin, dies of a cocaine seizure. Chris succumbs to peer pressure and begins using first marijuana and then cocaine. Finally, Tina is shown saying she can quit taking crack, but not too convincingly.

Reviewed in *School Library Journal*, July 1989.

NF

Harris, Jonathan. **Drugged Athletes: The Crisis in American Sports.** New York: Four Winds Press, 1987. 192p. glossary. index. $12.95. LC 86-29396. ISBN 0-02-742740-4.

Professional athletes, cultural heroes to much of the population and role models for youth aspiring to fame and fortune, may be no worse substance abusers than members of their wide audiences. Yet, their very media exposure gives wide coverage to their problems. From steroids for body building to drugs to reduce or alleviate pain, increased use of all types of drugs has led to increased drug addiction. The author thoroughly covers the problems associated with stress, playing to win, the outcome of high salary, and the relation of gambling to winning. The book is very detailed, perhaps with too much repetition.

Reviewed in *Booklist*, July 1987; *Science Books and Films*, May/June 1988; and *VOYA*, October 1987.

NF
Hawkes, Nigel. **The Heroin Trail.** New York: Gloucester Press, 1986. 32p. illus. index. (Issues, Issues, Issues Series) $10.90. LC 86-80627. ISBN 0-531-17028-4. (GR 5-8)

This oversize book begins with a two-page photograph of an addict administering a shot of heroin. Illustrated with both color and black-and-white pictures, short chapters describe how users become addicted to both prescription and non-prescription drugs. Describing heroin from its growing fields to the marketplace, the book shows the impact heroin has on both the individual and the economy of this country and the world.

Reviewed in *Booklist*, January 1, 1987.

NF
Hawksley, Jane. **Teen Guide to Pregnancy, Drugs, and Smoking.** New York: Watts, 1989. 64p. $11.90. LC 89-31845. ISBN 0-531-1-835-X. (GR 9-12)

Illegal and commonly abused drugs, prescription drugs, over-the-counter medicines, caffeine, alcohol, and AIDS from intravenous drug use are placed in the context of pregnancy. A glossary of terms is followed by a list of the drugs that should never be taken by a pregnant woman. Because of its number of pages and the easy-to-read format, this book will be appealing to most readers who are not looking for a longer volume with a more difficult vocabulary.

Reviewed in *Booklist*, January 1, 1990.

NF
Hawley, Richard. **Think About Drugs and Society: Responding to an Epidemic.** New York: Walker, 1988. 157p. charts. photos. appendixes. bibliog. glossary. index. (Think Series) $18.85. LC 87-21681. ISBN 0-8027-6749-4. (GR 8-12)

The introduction discusses the drug problem and what is meant by a "drug," why there is a drug-abuse epidemic now, and whether drug use can be controlled. Chapter 2 includes the history of three intoxicating drugs—alcohol, cannabis, and cocaine. Drug use is traced and the pros and cons of important contemporary issues are outlined. The ways both individuals and the society respond to the problem of drug use are presented. Chapter 3 is titled "Contemporary Debate" and poses such questions as "Whose business is drug taking?" and "Is drug use a victimless crime?" Chapter 4 presents the future outlook. Appendixes include a list of ways to become involved with the issue; a list of organizations with a brief explanation of their activities and their addresses; "Two Voices in the Marijuana Debate"; the National Institute on Drug Abuse Report for 1987, "Danger Signals of Drug Abuse"; "The Single Convention on Narcotic Drugs" (1961); a forty-two-term glossary; and a five-page bibliography under general topics, special topics, articles, and film and video recordings.

NF
Henningfield, Jack E., and Nancy A. Ator. **Barbiturates: Sleeping Potion or Intoxicant.** New York: Chelsea House, 1986. 95p. illus. index. (The Encyclopedia of Psychoactive Drugs) $18.95. LC 85-17432. ISBN 0-87754-768-8.

This book describes barbiturates, how they work, their effects, medical uses, risks of barbiturate therapy, other risks, and how barbiturates are abused. Treating barbiturate abuse and overdose is detailed. Appendixes include a glossary of forty street terms related to barbiturates with the trade names or descriptions, a list of state agencies for the prevention and treatment of drug abuse, a general glossary of thirty-six terms, and a four-item reading list.

NF
Henningfield, Jack E. **Nicotine: An Old-Fashioned Addiction.** New York: Chelsea House, 1985. 143p. illus. (The Encyclopedia of Psychoactive Drugs) $17.95. LC 84-14956. ISBN 0-877-54751-3.

Information is given on the physiological and psychological effects of smoking. Reasons are outlined for why people smoke and treatments are suggested for quitting this form of drug addiction. Chapter titles include "Tobacco's Past," "What Is in Tobacco Smoke?," "Tobacco and Health," "Smoking, Women, and Pregnancy," "The Scientific Study of Cigarette Smoking Behavior," "Effects of Nicotine," "Are Tobacco and Nicotine Addicting?," "Tobacco and the Law," and "The Treatment of Cigarette Smokers." The appendix includes "Tolerance Questionnaire," "Further Help on Quitting Smoking," "Testimony to Congress," "Federal Trade Commission Estimates," "Research Strategies in Cigarette Smoking," and state agencies for the prevention and treatment of drug abuse.

FLM/VHS
Heroin and Human Physiology. Van Nuys, CA: AIMS Media, 1988. 22 min. film, $495.00; video, $395.00. Teacher's guide. (GR 7-12)

The painting of a twenty-four-year-old junkie, dead from an overdose, introduces this presentation of heroin as a medical opiate, terms and forms of street heroin, and the effects of heroin on the body. The information is interrupted by testimony from four recovering addicts. The risk of contracting AIDS through addiction is treated briefly as well as the effect on a baby when the mother is a user.

Reviewed in *School Library Journal*, May 1989.

VHS
High On Life: Feeling Good Without Drugs. Mount Kisco, NY: Guidance Associates, 1988. 46 min. video. $189.00. guide.

Brief testimonies by eight teenagers point out alternatives to drugs. Some perform before an audience, as dancers or athletes, while one is a rock climber. The music background and the charm of the speakers will keep the attention of the viewers. Some of the teenagers have had experience with drugs and other discouraging events. The video closes with a wheelchair athlete giving pointers on goal setting.

Reviewed in *Booklist*, June 15, 1988.

NF

Hofmann, Frederick G. **A Handbook on Drug and Alcohol Abuse: The Biomedical Aspects.** 2d ed. New York: Oxford University Press, 1983. 329p. bibliog. index. $25.00; $19.95 pa. LC 82-18930. ISBN 0-19-503056-7; 0-19-503056-5 pa.

This excellent book, written by a professor of pharmacology, has been revised to include some new material. The first edition was very well received. The work provides a comprehensive source of information about drugs that are commonly abused, and the discussions are very well written. An attempt is made to separate facts from fiction. Hofmann discusses such issues as why people start using drugs in the first place; why some abstain from use or abandon drugs after preliminary experimentation; whether LSD or marijuana causes chromosomal damage and birth defects; and whether we need stricter laws or some kind of legalization of drug use. Major emphasis is on the clinical effects of drug use on human beings.

The following topics are covered: (1) introduction, (2) some general aspects of drug abuse, (3) narcotic drugs, (4) generalized depressants of the central nervous system: alcohol, barbiturates and other drugs exerting similar effects, (5) generalized depressants of the central nervous system: volatile solvent and aerosol inhalation ("glue sniffing"), (6) hallucinogens: LSD, phencyclidine, and other agents having similar effects, (7) hallucinogens: marijuana, hashish, and atropinic drugs, (8) central nervous system stimulants, (9) the medical diagnosis of drug abuse, (10) management of selected clinical problems: pharmacological aspects, and (11) drug abuse and the law.

Chapters 9 and 10 present some very practical information on the medical diagnosis of drug abuse and the management of certain problems. The last chapter, which considers the legal aspects of the drug problem, is also notable, pointing out very good and not-often-mentioned reasons for not legalizing marijuana, at least at the present time: not enough is known about the consequences of various patterns of usage; the potency of marijuana varies; it is difficult to analyze the material or even describe it in regard to its composition; and it is possible to determine the active principles of marijuana (or metabolites of them) in blood only with the resources of a modern research laboratory.

This book is highly recommended for students and practitioners of the health professions particularly, but it is also suitable for educators and others who may be interested, at least with the help of a medical dictionary.

VHS

How to Say No without Losing Your Friends. Mount Kisco, NY: Guidance Associates, 1988. 60 min. video. $209.00

Peer pressure can confuse and wear down any teenager. Now here's a unique live-action video that does more than say why it's important not to give in to the crowd. It offers a practical course—full of valuable how-to techniques to make it easier to resist.

Students will learn how to speak up for themselves effectively, withstand pressure from their peers, and get themselves out of uncomfortable and even dangerous situations while maintaining friendships. A powerful practical program to help students learn skills and keep friends who will last a lifetime.

NF
Hughes, Barbara. **Drug-Related Diseases.** New York: Watts, 1987. 96p. illus. $9.90. (A First Book Series) LC 87-8140. ISBN 0-531-1038-1. (GR 4-9)

A number of drugs are presented including alcohol, cocaine, heroin, and amphetamines. The health problems that may result from the use or abuse of these drugs are given.

Reviewed in *Booklist*, January 1, 1988.

NF
Hutchings, Donald. **Methadone: Treatment for Addiction.** New York: Chelsea House, 1985. 112p. illus. index. bibliog. (The Encyclopedia of Psychoactive Drugs) $17.95. LC 85-7915. ISBN 0-877-54760-2.

Methadone treatment is described as "A New Choice, a New Hope." This drug is explored in a variety of perspectives including the historical use as an opiate "cure," maintenance programs, and alternatives. Chapters include "History of the Opiates," "Getting Hooked on Heroin," "The Effect of Heroin and Methadone on Pregnancy," "A Closer Look at Methadone Maintenance," "The 'New Solution' Spreads," "Learning from the Past," "Alternatives to the Methadone Maintenance," and "The Dilemma of Polydrug Abuse." The dangers of drugs to the unborn infant are stressed. Results of a five-year study of methadone maintenance showed that this substitute drug failed to halt returns to addiction. Further, the book reports that the treatment itself has become a problem. Finally a young executive's testimony is reported. An appendix includes a list of state agencies for the prevention and treatment of drug abuse, "Further Reading," and a glossary of thirty-seven terms.

Reviewed in *Book Report*, January-February 1989.

NF
Hyde, Margaret. **Alcohol: Uses and Abuses.** Hillside, NJ: Enslow, 1988. 96p. $13.95. glossary. index. LC 87-12161. ISBN 0-89490-155-9. (GR 7-12)

The social effects of drinking alcoholic beverages and the medical effects on the body are described. The disease of alcoholism is discussed as it affects the community in which alcoholics live. Hypothetical case studies are given to present information on how to get help for the alcoholic and how to get help as children of alcoholics through Al-Anon/Alateen. How to react in social situations as the child of an alcoholic and ways to resist peer pressure to drink alcoholic beverages are presented.

Reviewed in *School Library Journal*, September 1988.

NF
Hyde, Margaret O. **Mind Drugs.** New York: Dodd, Mead, and Co., 1986. 191p. glossary. index. illus. $10.95. LC 86-11487. ISBN 0-396-08813-9. (GR 7-12)

In this fifth edition of Margaret Hyde's book, leading authorities on drugs update the use and misuse of a variety of mind-altering drugs. New terms such as "designer drugs" have been added. Findings by the medical profession on the long-term effects of marijuana, alcohol, LSD, heroin, cocaine, PCP, and other drugs are discussed by six different authors, all authorities. Experimental alternatives to drug use are described. Readers are warned of the dangers of contracting AIDS from shared needles. Driving and drinking or using drugs is discussed with information about Students Against Driving Drunk. The book offers methods that teens can use to get drunk drivers off the highways. A copy of the SADD contract is reproduced in an appendix. Drug charts list drug names, uses, physiological and psychological dependence, tolerance, duration of effect, methods of administration, and the effects of psychoactive drugs.

Reviewed in *School Library Journal*, November 1986, and *VOYA*, February 1987.

VHS/FS

If Someone in Your Family Drinks. Pleasantville, NY: Sunburst Communications, 1987. 23 min. video, $139.00; filmstrip, $119.00. (GR 6-8)

A good example of still pictures from filmstrips reproduced as a moving picture through cuts, dissolves, pans, and zooms of still pictures. This presentation features children of alcoholics and describes the possibility of their becoming alcoholics. The scene is a group of students discussing the alcoholism in their homes with the school counselor. The suggestion is made that these students should watch or change their behavior and also that organizations such as Alateen can be helpful.

Reviewed in *Booklist*, September 1, 1988.

VHS

Intervention: Facing Reality. Minneapolis, MN: The Johnston Institute, 1989. 30 min. video. $525.00.

Narrated by Hugh Downs, this is the third in a series including *Back to Reality* and *Enabling: Masking Reality.* The video demonstrates that intervention is the first step toward recovery for everyone in the life of an addict. Bringing addicts and the people in their lives who matter most to them face-to-face with reality is essential. This video was winner of the Bronze Apple Award of the National Educational Film and Video Festival.

NF

Isralowitz, Richard, and Mark Singer, eds. **Adolescent Substance Abuse: A Guide to Prevention and Treatment.** New York: Haworth Press, 1983. 123p. bibliog. index. (Child and Youth Services: Vol. 6, No. 1/2) $22.95. LC 83-13015. ISBN 0-86656-185-4.

Because of the prevalence and effects of drug and alcohol use among teenagers, interest in the matter has increased dramatically over the past decade. Consequently there has been a surge of research efforts and an increase in services for chemically dependent youth. The purpose of this work is to encourage further exploration by presenting articles which may lend a new perspective to the field or which discuss aspects of the problem that have not received enough attention. The eight papers are by experts (most in the social science field) who have included scholarly bibliographies with their contributions but who write in a manner understandable to the general public.

NF
Jackson, Michael, and Bruce Jackson. **Doing Drugs.** New York: St. Martin's Press, 1983. 320p. A St. Martin's/Marek Book. $7.95 pa. LC 82-17035. ISBN 0-312-21615-7.

The authors of this book are father and son. To gather the material presented, the son, Michael, nineteen, interviewed a number of young people he considered typical upper-middle-class youths about their experiences with drugs. Their case histories are recorded. The view taken by the authors is that parents haven't the slightest idea what their children are doing. Most parents use drugs themselves (although legal ones, usually, such as alcohol and prescription drugs). The book makes it evident that parents and their children do not communicate well.

The work is in three parts. The first consists of interviews and conversations on drug use with six of Michael's friends. Part 2, "Practical Matters," is extracts from interviews broken down by what seemed to be the major matter of concern, such as how one starts using drugs or relations with other people. Part 3 is about one teenager who succumbed totally to drugs. A variety of types are treated in the book, from youths who do not use drugs at all (a few only) to the one who was a hopeless addict.

The aim of the book is to give parents and young people a perspective on the extent and nature of the drug abuse problem today. Perhaps it can also promote some understanding between them.

NF
Johanson, Chris-Ellyn. **Cocaine: A New Epidemic.** New York: Chelsea House, 1986. 107p. illus. index. (The Encyclopedia of Psychoactive Drugs) $17.95. LC 85-25969. ISBN 0-877-54765-3.

Cocaine is described in this book as "the New Epidemic." Indeed the use of cocaine and its derivatives has reached epidemic proportions. The chapters describe what cocaine is, its effects on the body, its chemical structure, history, patterns, and trends of use, scientific studies, and new treatments for abusers. Appendixes include a list of state agencies for the prevention of drug abuse, a six-item bibliography, and a glossary of fifty-six terms.

NF
Johnston, Lloyd D., Patrick M. O'Malley, and Jerald G. Bachman. **Drugs and American High School Students 1975-1983.** Rockville, MD: National Institute on Drug Abuse, [1984]. DHHS Publication No. (ADM) 85-1374.

The research for this report was conducted at the Institute for Social Research at the University of Michigan with funding from the National Institute on Drug Abuse. The research design and procedures are given, followed by an overview of the key findings. More lengthy reports are given on the prevalence of drug abuse with a summary of all drugs and specific reports on marijuana/hashish, inhalants, hallucinogens, cocaine, heroin, other opiates, stimulants, sedatives, tranquilizers, alcohol, and cigarettes. Then-current attitudes, beliefs, and social milieu are also reported. The date of this research would make it very useful for comparative studies at the present time.

NF
Jones, Ralph. **Straight Talk, Answers to Questions Young People Ask About Alcohol.** new ed. Blue Ridge Summit, PA: Tab Books, 1988. 88p. $4.95 pa. LC 89-4349. ISBN 0-8306-9005-0. (GR 7-12)

The author has made presentations at schools for many years. This book includes the answers to questions asked by the audience, presenting facts in the question-answer format, arranged by subject. A bibliography is included and places to seek help are listed. Its easy-to-read format will appeal to the older reader with fewer reading skills.

Reviewed in *Book Report*, January-February 1990.

NF
Jussim, Daniel. **Drug Tests and Polygraphs: Essential Tools or Violations of Privacy?** New York: Messner, 1987. 116p. $11.29; $5.95 pa. LC 87-11192. ISBN 0-671-64438-6, 0-671-65977-4 pa. (GR 9-up)

This book describes how drug tests and the less-known but related polygraphs are administered, how the tests work, and how the results are being used. Drug testing is presented in private business, the school, and the government. The reader is questioned about the legal aspects: is drug testing a violation of due process and the right to privacy? Accuracy of drug tests is a major problem today. Court cases that have used the results of drug testing and polygraphs are cited.

Reviewed in *Booklist*, September 1, 1988.

NF
Kaplan, John. **The Hardest Drug: Heroin and Public Policy.** Chicago: University of Chicago Press, 1985. 248p. bibliog. index. (Studies in Crime and Justice) $10.95 pa. LC 82-17514. ISBN 0-226-42427-8.

The author of this work is a professor of law. He has written an excellent analysis of heroin as a social problem, and offered as good a solution as can probably be found among unattractive policy alternatives. He explores costs and benefits of different policies toward heroin.

Kaplan's view is that people take heroin because they like to, not because pushers get them addicted. Peer pressure and the wish for status are the culprits. It is not necessarily true, he says, that "once an addict always an addict." Addicts sometimes abstain and may or may not become readdicted. He does not believe addiction is a disease. He thinks we should try to control heroin addiction because it leads to property crime and welfare payments.

As for treatment, Kaplan thinks therapeutic communities are not very successful and are expensive. They work only as long as the addict remains in the community. He feels that replacement of heroin addiction by controlled methadone addiction is the most promising of treatments. Kaplan thinks criminal addicts, by switching to methadone maintenance, can stabilize their lives. He would ignore nonaddict noncriminal users (there are some). He closes by saying that "if the heroin problem were an easy one, we probably would have solved it by now."

The book is clearly written and understandable to the average young reader.

NF

Keigley, Peggy. **Quit and Win: The War of Cigarette Withdrawal Once and For All.** Schenectady, NY: PBK Publications, 1987. 109p. appendix. $9.95 pa. LC 87-90483. ISBN 0-94228-00-X. (GR 9-12)

A former smoker, this author provides guidelines and a variety of strategies for persons who wish to quit smoking. These include setting a target date, keeping aware of the physiological impact, and dealing with friends who do not help the cause of quitting and winning.

Reviewed in *Booklist*, December 15, 1987.

NF

Ketcham, Katherine, and Ginny Lyford Gustafson. **Living on the Edge: A Guide to Intervention for Families with Drug and Alcohol Problems.** New York: Bantam, 1989. 259p. bibliog. $8.95 pa. LC 88-7723. ISBN 0-553-34606-7. (GR 9-12)

One of the authors, an experienced intervention counselor, works from the premise that "the better way is to help the family members change *their* lives." Families need help before they are destroyed. The book is divided into three parts: Identifying, Understanding, and Overcoming. Selection from the twenty-eight chapter titles include "Whose Problem Is This, Anyway?," "Learning to Live in the Here and Now," "The Survival Roles," "Can You Love Too Much?," "How Long Do You Hang On?," "Finding a Counselor," "Dealing with the Real World," "Getting the Facts Down," and "Looking Ahead." The appendix includes thirty-two pages of "Drug Facts" listing various drugs and their medical uses, primary effects, addiction potential, symptoms of addiction, withdrawal symptoms, and causes of death, plus a fourteen-item reading list, and a National Substance Abuse Resources list.

This work offers "no-nonsense advice on how to recognize and treat chemical addiction." It is a how-to guide for intervention. *Living on the Edge* explains how the family, with the aid of an addiction counselor, confronts the addicted member and convinces him or her to seek treatment. Also included in the work are concise examples of actual interventions, guidelines for conducting an intervention, and what to do if the intervention fails.

VHS

Kevin's Story II. Producer: Ginny Durrin. Washington, D.C.: Durrin Productions, 1989. 26 min. video. $390.00 (GR 8-adult)

This is part II in the history of Kevin Tunnel who was sentenced for drunk driving and causing a fatal accident. He serves as a speaker with two other recovering alcoholics to get the audience to weigh peer pressures, parental pressures, and advertising to determine whether to become substance abusers. The possibility of genetic predisposition to substance abuse and ways to say no are presented, along with the problems of teenage pregnancy.

Reviewed in *Booklist*, January 1, 1990.

NF
Keyishian, Elizabeth. **Everything You Need to Know about Smoking.** New York: Rosen, 1989. 64p. index. glossary. bibliog. illus. $12.95. LC 89-10256. ISBN 0-8239-1017-2.

A discussion of the dangerous effects of smoking, this book includes information on why people start and why it is so hard to quit. Suggestions are given on how to quit smoking.

NF
Kinney, Jean, and Gwen Leaton. **Understanding Alcohol.** New York: New American Library, and St. Louis, MO: C. V. Mosby Co., 1982. 270p. illus. bibliog. index. (Mosby Medical Library: A Plume Book) $8.95 pa. LC 81-22557. ISBN 0-452-25338-1.

Published as a joint venture by C. V. Mosby Company and the New American Library, this book is one of a new series of medical books suitable for laypersons. It is a revised version of a work published in 1978, *Loosening the Grip: A Handbook of Alcohol Information.* The latter was intended as a text for alcoholism trainees or other professional workers who dealt with alcohol problems, but it became popular with the public also. This more recent edition contains much the same material, but it focuses more broadly on problems encountered by all those whose lives are touched by alcoholism in one way or another.

The book presents a great deal of basic material and provides an overview of the issues involved in alcoholism treatment. It synthesizes information in the fields of medicine, psychology, psychiatry, sociology, anthropology, and counseling that applies to alcohol abuse and treatment. In addition to material on treatment, the following topics are considered: history of alcohol use; theories on drinking and the etiology of alcoholism; guidelines for diagnosis of alcoholism; effects of alcohol on the body and behavior; effects of alcoholism on the family; effects on special populations such as women, adolescents, and the aged; complications associated with alcoholism; and where the alcoholic can go for help. Scattered throughout the work in the margins are apt cartoons and captions.

The work can be described as a practical guide or handbook as well as a pool of knowledge about alcoholism.

FIC
Klein, Norma. **Learning How to Fall.** New York: Bantam, 1989. 192p. $13.95. LC 88-37145. ISBN 0-553-05809-6. (GR 10-12)

This novel has as its major focus the mental health of a seventeen-year-old, Dustin Penrose. This hero's father, a recovering alcoholic, has his son committed to a private mental facility when Dustin's relationship with his girlfriend, Star McEnnis, causes Dustin emotional stress. Explicit language and unorthodox sexual activities are found in the volume.

Reviewed in *School Library Journal*, June 1989.

NF
Knox, Jean McBee. **Drinking, Driving, and Drugs.** New York: Chelsea House, 1988. 112p. illus. (The Encyclopedia of Psychoactive Drugs) $17.95. LC 87-27733. ISBN 1-555-46231-6.

The impact of various psychoactive drugs on the ability to drive is described in this book. The tragic outcomes are shown with examples of the consequences of teenagers who drink and drive, examining in detail the victims, the drivers, alcoholism, and the laws. The technology and the whys and hows of catching drunk drivers are also examined. Two appendixes are provided, one describing the progressive severity of punishments for driving under the influence (DUI) of alcohol and the other listing state agencies for the prevention and treatment of drug abuse.

Reviewed in *Booklist*, July 1988.

NF

Knox, Jean McBee. **Drugs throughout the Ages.** New York: Chelsea House, 1987. 106p. illus. (The Encyclopedia of Psychoactive Drugs) $17.95. LC 86-26885. ISBN 1-555-46221-9.

The volume is an exploration of the history of man's use of drugs that alter consciousness. Chapters include "Prehistory and Ancient History," "The Middle Ages: 476-1400," "The Age of Discovery: 1440-1750," "The Scientific Age, Part I: 1750-1870," "The Scientific Age, Part II: 1870-1920," "The 20th Century," and "Future Ages." The appendix includes a list of state agencies for the prevention and treatment of drug abuse and a glossary with twenty-nine terms.

FIC

Knopp, Paul. **Dope Deal.** St. Paul, MN: EMC Publishing, 1982. 96p. illus. (Encounter Series) $3.95 pa. LC 81-9766. ISBN 0-88436-818-1.

In this large-print novel for juveniles, Brian has been involved with drug dealers and is arrested for minor drug trafficking. He realizes that his former actions have had disastrous effects on himself and on his family and decides to cooperate with the police. With their help and the help of a friend, he saves his brother and himself from serious trouble with a drug-dealing motorcycle gang.

NF

Kokin, Morris, and Ian Walker. **Women Married to Alcoholics: Help and Hope for Nonalcoholic Partners.** New York: Morrow, 1989. 211p. $17.95. LC 89-8248. ISBN 0-688-08154-1.

A book to help dispel the myth that women are responsible for the behavior of their spouses when they are alcoholics. The authors scorn the term "codependent" as negative terminology. With case studies, the problems of women as partners of alcoholics are discussed.

Reviewed in *Booklist*, August 1989.

NF

The Koppel Report: A National Town Meeting; The Legalization of Drugs. American Broadcasting Co., September 13, 1988. 40p. $5.00 per copy. Transcript produced by Journal Graphics, Inc., 167 Broadway, New York, NY 10007.

The transcription of a television broadcast features Ted Koppel, William von Raab, William F. Buckley, Kurt Schmoke, Ethan Nadelmann, Jesse Jackson, Edward I. Koch, Henk Jan Van Vliet, Alan Dershowitz, Mitchell Rosenthal, Timothy Johnson, Shirley Thornton, Charles Rangel, Robert Stutman, Hugh Downs, and Jerome Jaffee. The final page of this booklet contains lists for other "Nightline," "ABC News Special," "20/20," and "ABC News Closeup" transcripts available from Journal Graphics.

NF

Kusinitz, Marc. **Drug Use around the World.** New York: Chelsea House, 1988. 160p. illus. (The Encyclopedia of Psychoactive Drugs) $17.95. LC 88-6140. ISBN 1-555-46233-2.

This volume presents the picture of problems of drug abuse from Europe, Africa, and the Far East as well as Latin America and North America. Chapters include "Alcohol Use and Abuse in North America," "Drug Abuse in North America," "Alcohol Use and Abuse in Europe," "Drug Abuse in Europe," "Use and Abuse in the Americas," "Use and Abuse in the Middle East and Africa," "Use and Abuse in Asia," and "Use and Abuse in Australia, New Zealand, and Polynesia." There is a bibliography and a glossary with forty-eight terms.

NF

Kusinitz, Marc. **Celebrity Drug Use.** New York: Chelsea House, 1988. 144p. illus. (The Encyclopedia of Psychoactive Drugs) $17.95. LC 87-6646. ISBN 1-555-46225-1.

An overt attempt is made in this book to deglamorize the celebrity-drug mystique. Almost biographical in nature, specific accounts are shown of celebrities who have successfully or unsuccessfully coped with a drug problem. This volume will have definite appeal for those who follow celebrities' lives. It includes all aspects of the entertainment world—music, theatre, movies, and comedy. This can be a very effective vehicle for drug awareness for star-struck teens. A reading list, glossary, and index are also included.

NF

Kusinitz, Marc. **Drugs and the Arts.** New York: Chelsea House, 1987. 124p. illus. (The Encyclopedia of Psychoactive Drugs) $17.95. LC 87-5179. ISBN 1-555-46224-3.

Drugs have made an impact, not only on athletes, but on creative professionals in dance, art, music, theatre, and motion pictures. This book also covers artistic works that portray the world of drugs and drug abuse. Chapter titles include "Drugs: The Lengthening Shadow," "Romanticism and Decadence," "Drugs and Jazz," "Drugs and Modern Literature," "Drugs on the Stage and Screen," "Drugs and Dance," and "Drugs, Painting, and Sculpture." The appendix includes a list of state agencies for the prevention and treatment of drug abuse and a glossary of forty-eight terms.

NF

Lamberg, Lynne. **Drugs and Sleep.** New York: Chelsea House, 1988. 128p. illus. (The Encyclopedia of Psychoactive Drugs) $17.95. LC 87-14582. ISBN 1-555-46213-8.

This volume is a story of the physiological and psychological reasons the body needs sleep. Further, the ways drugs, therapies, changes in eating, or behavioral patterns manipulate this crucial function are presented. Chapters include "The Nature of Sleep," "What Causes Insomnia?," "How Sleeping Pills Work," "Sleeping Pills: Uses and Types," "Food and Mood," "Good Sleep Habits," "Help for Troubled Sleepers," and "New Directions in Research." The appendix includes "For More Information," "Sleep/Wake Diary," "Sleepiness/Alertness Chart," a list of state agencies for the prevention and treatment of drug abuse, and a glossary with twenty-nine terms.

NF

Lang, Alan R. **Alcohol: Teenage Drinking.** New York: Chelsea House, 1985. 142p. illus. (The Encyclopedia of Psychoactive Drugs) $17.95. LC 85-7826. ISBN 0-877-54761-0.

The special focus of this volume is on alcohol problems of teenagers. Chapters include "Alcohol and Its History in America," "Expectations about Alcohol and Its Effects," "Short and Long-Term Effects," "Social Psychology and Drinking Behavior," "Patterns of Alcohol Consumption," "Drinking Problems of Teenagers," and "Alcohol and Public Policy." There is much overlap with another book in this series, *Alcohol and Alcoholism.* The appendix includes a list of state agencies for the prevention and treatment of drug abuse and an eleven-item bibliography.

NF

Langone, John. **Bombed, Buzzed, Smashed, or ... Sober: A Book About Alcohol.** New York: Avon Books, 1976. 160p. index. $14.95. LC 76-8490. ISBN 0-380-43653-1.

The history, use, abuse, causes, and effects of drinking are discussed in this work, as is treatment for alcoholism. The author attempts to supply the necessary information to produce a generation of responsible drinkers; abstinence is not stressed. Statistical data are included throughout the book, sometimes making for dull reading, but reader participation is encouraged through questions, quizzes, and a section on teenage dilemmas.

NF

Lee, Essie E. **Breaking the Connection: How Young People Achieve Drug-Free Lives.** New York: Messner, 1988. 156p. charts. photos. appendixes. index. $10.29; $5.95 pa. LC 87-18586. ISBN 0-671-63637-5, 0-672-67059-X pa. (GR 7-up)

Case studies of eight teens who have substance-abuse lifestyles but have begun intervention programs present how addiction can be broken. The current drug epidemic is shown and various treatment programs are described. This book also shows the effect of substance abuse on other members of the family.

Reviewed in *VOYA*, October 1988.

NF

Legal Issues for Alcohol and Other Drug Use Prevention and Treatment Programs Serving High-Risk Youth. Rockville, MD: U.S. Department of Health and Human Services, Public Health Service, 1990. OSAP Technical Report No. 2. Free.

Prepared by the Office for Substance Abuse, this volume is intended to provide authoritative guidance on legal issues facing alcohol and other drug treatment and prevention programs serving high-risk youth. Contents include when confidential information may be shared with others, questions and answers in applying the regulations, the right to treatment and parental consent, child abuse and neglect, reporting, screening potential employees and volunteers, and quality of care. A one-page checklist is available to use when "consulting with a knowledgeable attorney." The appendix includes a summary of state parental consent laws for the treatment of minors.

NF

Leite, Evelyn, and Pamela Espeland. **Different Like Me: A Book for Teens Who Worry About Their Parents' Use of Alcohol/Drugs.** Minneapolis, MN: Johnson Institute Books, 1987. 120p. illus. $6.95. LC 86-33818. ISBN 0-935908-34-X. (GR 7-up)

Information is given about chemical dependence—what it is and what it does to users. The book makes suggestions to and offers advice for teens with alcohol- or drug-dependent parents. The point is made that children with parents who have problems with substance abuse should stop feeling "different" and start feeling "good." A list of organizations to seek assistance is provided.

Reviewed in *VOYA*, October 1987.

NF

Levy, Stephen J. **Managing the "Drugs" in Your Life: A Personal and Family Guide to the Responsible Use of Drugs, Alcohol, Medicine.** New York: McGraw-Hill, 1983. 330p. bibliog. index. $16.95. LC 82-24951. ISBN 0-07-037411-2.

The author of this popular work begins by saying that ours is a drug-taking society. His book is based on these premises: (1) drugs have become an integral part of life in modern America, (2) drugs are neither good nor bad but have abuse potential depending on who uses them and how, (3) we must assume full responsibility for what we put in our bodies and, conversely, we must not abdicate this responsibility to others, and (4) a core of practical wisdom is already at hand to aid in making informed decisions about the drugs we use. The main purpose of the book is to share some concepts and warnings that will guide the reader in the decision-making process concerning drug use.

The book covers the entire field of drugs, not just those commonly abused. There are five main sections: "Drugs and the Family," "Drugs and School," "Drugs and the Workplace," "Drugs as Medicine," and "Getting High." There are, in addition, several useful appendixes: "A Summary of Drug Information," "Additional Readings," "Where to Get Help," and "The Marijuana Laws."

The book is interesting to read, presents authentic information, and gives good advice. For instance, the author says denial that anything can happen to us is responsible for more deaths in the drug scene than anyone cares to acknowledge. "What about Natalie Wood and William Holden? And Janis Joplin, Jimi Hendrix, John Belushi, Marilyn Monroe, Elvis Presley, and many, many others? Richard Pryor is reported to have almost burned to death while free-basing cocaine." Such tragedies could have been prevented.

NF

Long, Robert Emmet, ed. **Drugs and American Society.** New York: H. W. Wilson Co., 1986. 206p. (*The Reference Shelf*: Vol. 57, No. 6) $10.00. LC 85-26604. ISBN 0-8242-0714-9.

A collection of articles reprinted from journals. These present drug trafficking and drug abuse in the United States at the present time. Parts include "International Drug Trafficking," "Cocaine," "Marijuana," and "Drugs and Celebrities." While the articles are, for the most part, from popular periodicals that would be found in the school's collection, it is helpful to have them in this single volume. Further, the editor's introduction to each part is very helpful in setting the stage for the articles that follow.

NF

Ludwig, Arnold M. **Understanding the Alcoholic's Mind: The Nature of Craving and How to Control It.** New York: Oxford University Press, 1988. 188p. bibliog. index. $16.95. LC 87-11328. ISBN 0-19-504878-4.

The author, a medical doctor, traces the "Paradoxes and Contradictions" from the moral, biological, social, and spiritual perspectives. The spiritual includes this: "10 percent of all AA recoveries happen through a 'rapid awakening' by either a true religious experience or a sweeping psychological event." He describes the "Lure of the Sirens," pointing out how alcoholics set themselves up for a relapse. Other chapters investigate "The Dry Drunk," "The Mystery of Craving," "On and Off the Wagon," "The Proper Frame of Mind," "Resisting Temptation," "Sobriety Scripts," and "The Sober Mind." Extensive notes further expand each chapter. The book stresses sobriety rather than treatment and discusses methods to control alcoholic craving through reducing the urge to drink.

NF

Lukas, Scott E. **Amphetamines: Danger in the Fast Lane.** New York: Chelsea House, 1985. 109p. illus. (The Encyclopedia of Psychoactive Drugs) $17.95. LC 85-476. ISBN 0-877-54755-6.

This book presents a broad picture of amphetamine use and abuse. Chapters include "History of Amphetamine Use and Abuse," "When Use Becomes Abuse," "Behavioral Effects of Amphetamines," "The Effects of Amphetamine on the Brain and Body," "Addiction to Amphetamines," "Amphetamine Psychosis," "Other Toxic Effects of Amphetamine," "Medical Uses of Amphetamine," and "Amphetamine and the Law." The book covers methods of detecting amphetamines in body fluids and unexpected toxic reactions. Appendixes include a discussion of amphetamine-related preparations, "If a Friend Is in Trouble with Amphetamine," case studies, a list of state agencies for the prevention and treatment of drug abuse, "Further Readings," and a glossary of eighty-one terms.

NF

McCormick, Michele. **Designer-Drug Abuse.** New York: Watts, 1989. 126p. diagrams. bibliog. (Impact Books) $12.90. LC 88-30450. ISBN 0-531-10660-8. (GR 7-12)

This author defines designer drugs as synthetic drugs combining synthetically produced chemicals as opposed to those with a plant base such as cocaine or heroin. Four drugs and their derivatives are the focus, including fentanyl, methamphetamine, PCP, and Ecstasy. The manufacture and distribution of these drugs is presented, along with some information concerning the history of laws related to controlled substances. Case studies describe the effects of these drugs and the possible outcomes of use such as overdose, permanent disability, and psychosis. Descriptions of the laboratories where they are manufactured contain information concerning the hazards of these drug factories.

Reviewed in *Booklist*, August 1989.

NF

McFarland, Rhonda. **Coping with Substance Abuse.** New York: Rosen Publications, 1987. 145p. index. (Coping Series) $12.95. LC 87-16537. ISBN 0-8239-0733-3. (GR 7-up)

This book describes the behavior of drug abusers and presents situations to help teenagers cope. Case studies in the book are fictionalized. The author, an alcoholism and drug abuse counselor, describes the impact of the chemically dependent on the family. Hopefully, they can gain insights into the disease of chemical dependency. Teens with an alcoholic parent are encouraged to seek help from Alateen rather than remain silent about the problem. In the case of drug dependency, readers are cautioned not to try to rescue, save, or fix friends or relatives on drugs. Includes a resource list.

Reviewed in *Booklist*, May 1, 1988.

NF

McLellan, Tom. **Escape from Anxiety and Stress.** New York: Chelsea House, 1986. 92p. illus. (The Encyclopedia of Psychoactive Drugs) $17.95. LC 85-31378. ISBN 0-877-54772-6.

The causes and consequences of stress are discussed as they relate to the use and abuse of drugs such as alcohol and marijuana. Major causes of stress include physical appearance and well-being, social situations and interpersonal relationships, school and job, and family relationships. Chapter titles include "Stress and Its Consequences," "Major Causes of Stress," "Early Emotional and Social Development," "The Emotions of Stress," "Drugs and the Nervous System," "Alcohol, Marijuana, Stimulants," and "Are Drugs Useful in Handling Stress?" The appendix includes a list of state agencies for the prevention and treatment of drug abuse, a nine-item bibliography, and a forty-seven-term glossary.

NF

Madison, Arnold. **Drugs and You.** Rev. ed. New York: Julian Messner, a division of Simon and Schuster, Inc., 1982. 96p. illus. index. $8.79. LC 82-3450. ISBN 0-671-43986-3.

Intended for young people in grades three through six, this book makes a strong case against the misuse of drugs. It is well illustrated with photographs. Following are the chapter headings: "The Drug List," "Basic Facts about Drugs," "The Use and Misuse of Drugs," "Drug Misuse and the Law," "Drug Abuse and Alcohol Addiction," "Alcohol, Caffeine, and Nicotine," "Glue-Sniffing," "Heroin and Other Narcotics," "Marijuana, LSD, Peyote, and Mescaline," "Depressants and Stimulants," "Controlling the Illegal Drug Traffic and Curing Drug Addiction," and "Drugs and You." Also included is a short glossary of terms relating to drug abuse.

The material has been suitably handled in a factual and not overly sensational manner. A teacher can benefit from use of the book because it contains ideas about how to approach class discussions on drug abuse.

FLM/VHS

Marijuana Alert. New York: Phoenix Films, 1982. 20 min. film, $415.00; video, $250.00.

This film presents recent results of research in the field on the physiological effects of marijuana. The drug is shown to be somewhat harmful to the organs of the human body suggesting that the viewers should take this into account when deciding whether or not to use marijuana.

NF

Marshall, Eliot. **Legalization: A Debate.** New York: Chelsea House, 1988. 121p. illus. photos. (The Encyclopedia of Psychoactive Drugs) $17.95. LC 87-23271. ISBN 1-555-46229-4.

This volume is another presenting the debate on whether drug use should be legalized or not. Chapters include "70 Years of Drug Prohibition," "Alcohol: The Legal Drug," "Drug Abuse Today: Trends and Consequences," "Illicit Drugs as Medicine," "The Case for Legalizing Marijuana Use," and "The Case for Prohibiting Marijuana Use." Appendix includes a list of state agencies for the prevention and treatment of drug abuse, a bibliography with eleven items, and a twenty-four-term bibliography.

NF

Martin, Jo, and Kelly Clendenon. **Drugs and the Family.** New York: Chelsea House, 1988. 97p. illus. (The Encyclopedia of Psychoactive Drugs) $17.95. LC 87-24258. ISBN 1-555-46220-0.

The effect of drug use on one individual, a teenage boy, is described from the start through addiction to the beginning of the road to recovery and normal health. Chapter titles include "Getting Acquainted," "The Start," "The First Time," "The Addiction," "The Way Home: A Picture Essay," "Toward the End," "The Last Straw," "The Beginning," and "The Road Back." The appendix includes a list of state agencies for the prevention and treatment of drug abuse.

NF

Meer, Jeff. **Drugs and Sports.** New York: Chelsea House, 1987. 132p. illus. photos. (The Encyclopedia of Psychoactive Drugs) $17.95. LC 87-753. ISBN 1-555-46226-X.

The author is currently an assistant editor at *Psychology Today.* His preface describes the shock of Len Bias's death from an overdose of cocaine when he was on the verge of becoming a professional athlete superstar. Chapter titles include "Alcohol, Nicotine, and Caffeine," "Marijuana and Cocaine," "Ergogenic Drugs," "Therapeutic Drugs," "Drug Testing," and "Treating Drug Abusers." The appendix contains a list of state agencies for the prevention and treatment of drug abuse, a bibliography with six items for further reading, and a glossary of forty-four terms.

FIC

Miklowitz, Gloria D. **Anything to Win.** New York: Delacorte, 1989. 138p. $11.95. LC 88-30909. ISBN 0-385-29750-5. (GR 7-12)

Steroid use is the subject of this novel, the story of a high school starting quarterback. The hero, Cam Potter, is small to play football and his coach wants him to gain thirty pounds. With the extra weight, Cam will be more attractive to college football scouts. A scholarship is the carrot; steroids, diet, and weight lifting are the solutions. Cam's behavior begins to change, and, as he becomes more aggressive, his girlfriend rejects him. Cam also finds himself with another side affect of steroid use, impotence. Finally, the trainer at the gymnasium, a long-term steroid user, is diagnosed as having cancer, and Cam stops using steroids.

Reviewed in *Book Report*, November-December 1989; *Booklist*, July 1989.

NF

Milgram, Gail Gleason. **Coping with Alcohol**, rev. ed. New York: Richard Rosen, 1987. 138p. illus. index. (Problem Solving Series) $12.95. LC 79-25817. ISBN 0-8239-0747-3. (GR 7-12)

Although this book is of most interest to young people, parents and educators can also make use of the information on alcohol, its use, effects, attendant problems, and ways to deal with it. The question-and-answer format is used after the introductory chapter in which the importance of clarifying values toward alcohol use is stressed. Sample exercises for this purpose are provided.

The following topics are dealt with: types of alcohol and alcoholic beverages, history of alcohol use, attitudes toward drinking, adult and teenage use, effects on the body, alcohol problems, alcoholism, and effects of alcoholism on family members. The rather simple presentation stresses the importance of making responsible decisions about alcohol use. The bibliography indicates audience level, and a list of resources for further information and a glossary are also included.

NF

Miller, Mark S. **Bad Trips.** New York: Chelsea House, 1988. 108p. illus. (The Encyclopedia of Psychoactive Drugs) $17.95. LC 87-14605. ISBN 1-555-46218-9.

The various drugs that can cause paranoia, hallucinations, and other unpleasant reactions are discussed. Mind-altering experiences that constitute "bad trips" are described in detail. Chapter titles include "Bad Trips—Then and Now," "Bad Trips: How They Happen," "Bad Trips and Mental Disorders," "Hallucinogens," "Narcotics," and "Sedative and Stimulants." The appendix includes a list of state agencies for the prevention and treatment of drug abuse and a glossary with forty-six terms.

NF

Miner, Jane C. **Alcohol and Teens.** New York: Messner, 1984. 63p. illus. (A Jem Book) $9.29. LC 84-658. ISBN 0-671-44890-0.

This book presents teenage drinking as a national problem. Case studies are given of teens who drink, teens who do not drink, and teens who have a drinking problem.

NF

Mohun, Janet. **Drugs, Steroids and Sports.** New York: Watts, 1988. 61p. illus. photos. $11.90. LC 88-50494. ISBN 0-531-10626-8. (GR 6-9)

Aimed at young athletes, this volume will appeal to the slow reader. Color photos of athletes from the United States and other countries who have lost their fame or their lives through the use of drugs, along with interesting quotations, will hold the interest of the athlete seeking information on this topic. The appendix discusses drug profiles, levels of addictiveness, and harmful side effects. Also included are addresses of thirteen organizations in the United States.

Reviewed in *School Library Journal*, May 1989.

NF
Molloy, J. Paul. **Self-Run, Self-Supported Houses for More Effective Recovery from Alcohol and Drug Addiction: Recovery, Responsibility, Replication.** Washington, D.C.: U.S. Department of Health and Human Services, Public Health Service. Office for Treatment Improvement, [1989]. Free.

Under the Anti-Drug Abuse Act of 1988 (P.L. 100-690), each state is required to establish revolving funds to provide small loans to individuals recovering from alcoholism or other drug addiction to start self-run, self-supported recovery houses. This "technical assistance" manual is designed for implementation of the act and would be useful information to explain the concept of this form of treatment. Appendixes include the effect of zoning laws on replication of Oxford Houses, and photographs and descriptions are given of Oxford Houses. The Oxford House manual, federal guidelines, the act, a model loan application, 1988 profile of Oxford House residents, and the program from a two-day conference held in August 1989 complete the book.

NF
Monroe, Judy. **Prescription Drugs.** Riverside, NJ: Crestwood House, 1988. 47p. $10.95. illus. (The Facts About Series) LC 88-22911. ISBN 0-89686-414-6. (GR 7-12)

One of a series of easy-reading, health-related books, this volume includes facts about the pharmaceutical industry, the drug-testing process, specific classes of familiar drugs, and information on how to become an informed consumer.

Reviewed in *Booklist*, April 1, 1989.

NF
Monroe, Judy. **Stimulants & Hallucinogens.** Riverside, NJ: Crestwood House, 1988. 47p. illus. (The Facts About Series) LC 88-20350. ISBN 0-89686-415-4. (GR 7-12)

Another in a series of easy-reading, health-related books, this volume is organized by type of drug—cocaine, crack, LSD, and caffeine—and focuses on the side effects of each. This book should appeal to the slower reader because of its illustrations, many photographs, and the presentation of the legality of drug use and the harmful effects rather than a moral approach.

NF
Morgan, Cynthia. **If You Love Somebody Who Smokes: Confessions of a Nicotine Addict.** Berkeley, CA: City Miner, 1987. 104p. $5.95 pa. LC 87-071061. ISBN 0-933944-14-4.

The author, a former smoker, details the problems associated with her struggle with giving up cigarettes. She also explains the cultural legacy of tobacco and the history of the development of the tobacco industry. An entertaining book that will keep the attention of the reader.

NF

National Directory of Drug Abuse and Alcoholism Treatment and Prevention Program. National Institute on Drug Abuse, 1989. OCLC. 370p. S/N 017-024-013633. $19.00. HE 20. 8302. D84.

Lists approximately 7,500 federal, state, local, and privately funded agencies responsible for the administration or provision of alcoholism or drug abuse services.

NF

Newman, Susan. **It Won't Happen to Me: True Stories of Teen Alcohol and Drug Abuse.** New York: Putnam Publishing Group, 1987. 128p. $8.95 pa. LC 86-25503. ISBN 0-399-51342-6.

The problems of alcohol and drug abuse among young people are illustrated with nine case histories.

NF

Newman, Susan. **You Can Say No to a Drink or a Drug.** New York: Perigee/Putnam, 1986. 128p. illus. $8.95. LC 86-464. ISBN 0-399-51228-4. (GR 4-9)

Illustrated with black-and-white photographs, this book presents scenarios of such potential teen drinking situations as a party in a home with the parents away, a recreational outing, the bowling alley, and babysitting. The situations are realistic with some happy and some less happy endings. Each story is followed by "You Should Know," a list of seven to ten items ("Most people don't realize that alcohol is a very powerful drug. Like cocaine, heroin, angel dust, and marijuana, alcohol alters how people think, feel, and act.") and "Keep in Mind," an additional seven to ten items ("If no adult is visible, ask if one is present. A party is less likely to get out of control when a parent is home.").

NF

Newton, Miller. **Gone Way Down: Teenage Drug-Use Is a Disease.** Tampa, FL: American Studies Press, 1981. 72p. illus. $2.95 pa. LC 81-524-11. ISBN 0-934996-16-4.

The author of this small book is the director of STRAIGHT, Inc., a drug rehabilitation program for adolescents in Florida. He hopes that his book will help parents and others involved with drug-using children find the knowledge necessary to overcome fear and act in the best interests of the young people. His view is that the adult world must say "no" to drug use. Newton became interested in helping drug abusers when he realized his own son had a drug problem.

The book begins with background materials, including a description of STRAIGHT, Inc. The next chapter deals with "drug-use" and "drug abuse" as concepts. Newton then explains that drug use is a disease of choice, and he deals with its characteristics. Next a comparison is made of addiction and habituation as drug-use processes, and drug use is described as a disease of the feelings. Several chapters are involved with the progressive stages of drug use. The last chapters discuss drug use as a family disease and offer hope that the condition is treatable. Parents are urged to take action, that is, to find effective programs and put their children in them.

NF
Peterson, Robert C., Sidney Cohen, F. R. Jeri, David E. Smith, and Lee I. Dogoloff. **Cocaine: A Second Look.** Washington, D.C.: American Council on Marijuana and Other Psychoactive Drugs, Inc., 1983. 46p. bibliog. $2.50 pa. LC 83-70823.

The council that produced this work is an organization dedicated to public education about the health hazards of various psychoactive substances. The council takes the view that public understanding of the consequences of use of these drugs is necessary to augment the efforts of families, communities, churches, and cultural and legal groups in dealing with drug abuse. The authors of the booklet are top experts in the field who ask the reader to take a second look at a dangerous drug that is a great deceiver and "should not be tried, even once."

Details on users and their treatment are provided. The impact of the new freebase method of smoking cocaine is covered, as are the effects of the coca paste epidemic in Peru. The last chapter discusses policy issues involved in the U.S. government's attempt to control the drug. The booklet ends with a plea to the media and the entertainment industry to realize that it is in the public interest to refrain from portraying cocaine as chic and "in," thereby encouraging its use. Otherwise we may relearn some of the painful lessons of history.

NF
Pittman, Bill. **AA, The Way It Began.** Seattle, WA: Glen Abbey Books, 1988. 239p. $8.95. LC 87-73390. ISBN 0-934125-08-2.

A history of the creation of Alcoholics Anonymous, the most successful of all self-help substance abuse groups and the biography of AA's founder, Bill Wilson. A history of alcohol treatment and study is also included.

Reviewed in *Booklist*, June 15, 1988.

NF
Pittman, Bill. **Stepping Stones to Recovery.** Seattle, WA: Glen Abbey Books, 1988. 282p. $8.95. LC 87-73389. ISBN 0-934125-04-X.

A collection of short essays and anecdotes written by alcoholics who have, through their association with Alcoholics Anonymous, recovered. This is written in the manner of a visit to an AA meeting.

Reviewed in *Booklist*, June 15, 1988.

VHS
Portrait of a Teenage Drug Abuser. Irwindale, CA: Barr Films, 1987. 23 min. (GR 7-12)

Six young people recount how they got into drugs, how it affected them, and how they feel during their present treatment.

NF
Pownell, Mark. **Inhalants.** New York: Watts, 1987. 62p. illus. (Understanding Drugs) $11.90. LC 87-50598. ISBN 0-531-10434-6. (GR 5-9)

This book discusses why persons use inhalants, the harmful effects of inhalants, and how individuals can seek help in overcoming this addiction.

Reviewed in *Booklist*, January 1, 1988; *School Library Journal*, February 1988.

VHS

Project Quit: The Moore Report, Where There's Smoke. Producer: Michael Mierendorf. Bloomington, IN: Indiana University Audiovisual Center, 1988. 56 min. video. $180.00. (GR 8-adult)

A documentary about the efforts of two businesses in Minnesota's Twin Cities area to stop smoking by their employees. The message is to resist beginning a psychologically and physically addictive habit.

Reviewed in *Booklist*, August 1989.

VHS

Real People: Meet a Teenage Drug Addict. Pleasantville, NY: Sunburst, 1988. 104p. 24 min. video, $139.00; filmstrip, $99.00. (GR 9-12)

This story of a white, middle class, female drug addict begins in high school with withdrawal from family and friends. Physical change is shown as well as psychological change, the latter through the switch from a cheerful drawing style to one featuring black, grey, and white faces. The heroine admits her addictive behavior and is treated in a hospital. She is now in college attending meetings of a support group.

Reviewed in *School Library Journal*, June 1989.

VHS

The Rehearsal: Understanding Addiction. Skokie, IL: Gerald T. Rogers Productions, 1989. 22 min. video. $350.00. (GR 9-12)

Using the ploy of a play rehearsal, the cast analyzes their characterizations. In discussing the performance, information is given on substance abuse and the effect on families. At the close of this video, a review is given of the basic information that was presented.

Reviewed in *School Library Journal*, September 1989.

VHS

Respect Yourself: Say No to Drugs. Mount Kisco, NY: Guidance Associates, 1988. 34 min. video. $175.00.

Interviews with four teenagers from diverse backgrounds and lifestyles show they have one thing in common: they've said no to drugs.

A guidance counselor gives specific suggestions on how not to go along with the crowd. And finally, teens from student organizations discuss the causes and effects of drug abuse, and the importance of saying no and believing it.

NF

Rice, Berkeley. **Trafficking: The Boom and Bust of the Air America Cocaine Ring.** New York: Scribner, 1989. 320p. $19.95. LC 89-10235. ISBN 0-684-19024-9.

The story of one entrepreneur from Scranton, Pennsylvania, Rik Luytjes, head of Air America, who organized a drug ring to fly tons of cocaine from Columbia. This group of "businessmen" made millions of dollars in the four years before they were caught.

Reviewed in *Booklist*, December 15, 1989.

NF

Richardson, P. Mick. **Flowering Plants: Magic in Bloom.** New York: Chelsea House, 1986. 121p. illus. index. (The Encyclopedia of Psychoactive Drugs) $18.95. LC 86-950. ISBN 0-87754-757-2.

Chapters include "Flowering Plants: Hallucinogens and Their Use," nutmeg, cannabis, cactus, Barbados cherry, morning glory, bean, and potato families as well as opium and cocaine. The history of the hallucinogens, their places of origin, and their uses are included. The appendix includes a list of state agencies for the prevention and treatment of drug abuse, eleven titles in a bibliography, and a seventy-one-term glossary.

FIC

Robinson, Mary. **Give It Up, Mom.** Boston: Houghton Mifflin, 1989. 176p. $13.95. LC 89-1767. ISBN 0-395-49700-0. (GR 5-7)

The heroine of this novel decides to encourage her mother to give up smoking for her seventh-grade Social Living class project. The premise that this project would "impact the world" is the first unlikely happening in the suspension of disbelief. However, the methods employed, including self-help groups, videotapes, and hypnosis, show that it is difficult to make an impact on another person's substance abuse.

Reviewed in *School Library Journal*, October 1989.

NF

Rodgers, Joann Ellison. **Drugs and Pain.** New York: Chelsea House, 1987. 142p. illus. (The Encyclopedia of Psychoactive Drugs) $17.95. LC 87-747. ISBN 1-555-46212-X.

The origins of different types of pain in the body are examined. This volume also discusses the various drugs and treatments that are available for pain relief. Chapter titles include "Pain: It's Mainly in the Brain," "Painkillers Then and Now," "Nonnarcotic Analgesics and Anesthetics," "Narcotics: The Link Between Pleasure and Pain," "Side Effects: Psychoactive and Otherwise," "Assessing Your Pain: How Much Does It Hurt?," "Where Does It Hurt? Teenage Pain," "Pain Relief Without Drugs," and "On the Horizon: New Methods of Pain Relief." The appendix includes a list of state agencies for the prevention and treatment of drug abuse, a selected list of pain relievers, a key to pronunciation, a sample pain diary, and a glossary of forty-six terms.

NF

Rodgers, Joann Ellison. **Drugs and Sexual Behavior.** New York: Chelsea House, 1988. 92p. illus. (The Encyclopedia of Psychoactive Drugs) $17.95. LC 87-23272. ISBN 1-555-46215-4.

The caption under one photograph states, "A young couple shares a marijuana joint. Early experimentation with drugs and sexual activity often go hand in hand. This is perhaps because both have the allure of the forbidden." Chapter titles include "Sexual Arousal," "Hormones: Nature's Own Drugs," "Aphrodisiacs: Fact or Fiction?," "Psychoactive Drugs and Sex," "Sexual Problems: Physiological and Psychological," and "Legitimate Drug Treatment and Sexual Therapy." The appendix includes a list of state agencies for the prevention and treatment of drug abuse, a thirteen-item reading list, and a glossary with forty-six terms.

NF

Roffman, Robert A. **Marijuana as Medicine.** Seattle, WA: Madrona Publishers, 1982. 180p. bibliog. index. $11.95; $8.95 pa. LC 82-6584. ISBN 0-914842-71-4; 0-914842-72-2 pa.

There is evidence that marijuana, or more precisely, some of the constituents of the plant, have medicinal value. Research on the matter is slowly taking place, although it is opposed by some because of the potential for misuse of the plant. Others are enthusiastic about the matter, evidently in the hope that the image of the plant will be improved if it is accepted as a medicament. The author of this book reviews the subject with what he feels is an unbiased view. His rationale for the book is that patients have a right to know and make decisions regarding their own treatment.

There are two main areas where marijuana has therapeutic potential: as treatment for glaucoma and in controlling the nausea associated with cancer chemotherapy. In the foreword, Dr. Sidney Cohen points out that marijuana is not a panacea. Chronic use of the plant has adverse consequences. In addition, there are already drugs for glaucoma, and marijuana does not ensure relief of the nausea and vomiting induced by cancer chemotherapy.

Chapter headings are: "The Law and the Debate," "Marijuana in History," "The Effects of Marijuana on Health and Behavior," "Research Studies on Marijuana and THC as Medicines," and "How to Use Marijuana." Chapter 2 includes an extensive table of penalties and sentences for marijuana possession or distribution, state by state. Chapter 4 has a table outlining recent research findings. The last chapter provides a few recipes for preparing marijuana for use in self-treatment. The book is suitable for the lay reader.

NF

Rosenberg, Maxine. **Not My Family: Sharing the Truth about Alcoholism.** New York: Bradbury, 1988. 80p. bibliog. $12.95. LC 88-10468. ISBN 0-02-777911-4. (GR 5-9)

Eight children and six adults narrate their experiences as children of alcoholics. Life is described in homes where the parent gave up drinking and in homes where the parent continued to drink. This book helps all preteens understand what life is like in this situation.

Reviewed in *Wilson Library Bulletin*, May 1989.

NF

Rucker, William B., and Marian E. Rucker, eds. **Drugs, Society and Behavior 87/88**, 2d ed. Guilford, CT: Dushkin Publishing, 1986. 241p. illus. index. LC 87-649280. ISBN 0-87967-682-5.

Books in Print lists a fourth edition of this in paperback, $9.95, ISBN 0-87967-784-8. However, the authors were only able to secure the second edition. This collection of articles from popular magazines is divided into six units with topic guides including "Topic: Drugs in Perspective," "Our Culture and the History of Drug Use," "Society vs. Drugs," "Topic: Drug Action on the Nervous System," "Transmitters and Receptors," "Endorphins and Beyond," "Topic: Drugs and Behavior," "Alcohol, Caffeine, and Tobacco," "Therapeutic Drugs: Psychiatric and Over-the-Counter Drugs," "Topic: Who Uses Psychotropic Drugs," "Personality and Drugs of Choice," "Lasting Changes from Drug Use," "Topic: Models of Dependency," "Biological and

Biochemical Models: The Disease Model," "Psychological and Social Models of Dependency," "Topic: Drug Abuse: Prevention and Treatment Issues," "Continuum of Care: Prevention," "Continuum of Care: Beyond Prevention," and "Natural Highs and Alternatives to Drugs." The topic guide uses fifty-two terms to direct the reader to the specific articles. A glossary of 192 terms is included.

NF

Ryan, Elizabeth A. **Straight Talk about Drugs and Alcohol.** New York: Facts on File, 1989. 144p. index. appendix. (Straight Talk for Teens Series) $14.95. LC 88-18050. ISBN 0-816-01525-2. (Age 13-up)

This book discusses the physical and social effects of drug and alcohol abuse, how to recognize addiction, and how to get help for dependency problems. Although substance abuse may have decreased in recent years, the problem remains. Because the emphasis of teens seems to be on alcohol abuse, the book emphasizes alcohol. The effects of drugs on specific parts of the body is explained. The book also includes a history of teen drug abuse in America. Special attention is paid to the pressures teenagers face, especially when their peer groups encourage the use and many adults set such very poor examples. The appendix is extensive, covering drug and alcohol facilities, Alcoholics Anonymous intergroups, Al-Anon and Alateen organizations, and state-by-state authorities and resources for further assistance, especially for teenagers who need help.

Reviewed in *Publishers Weekly*, November 25, 1988; *School Library Journal*, May 1989; and *Wilson Library Bulletin*, May 1989.

NF

Ryerson, Eric. **When Your Parent Drinks Too Much: A Book for Teenagers.** New York: Facts on File Publications, 1985. 144p. index. $14.95. LC 85-12961. ISBN 0-8160-1259-8. Warner Books, 1987. 192p. $3.95. pa. ISBN 0-446-34692-6.

The author lived for eleven years with his alcoholic mother, an existence with a sense of isolation that a loving father, brother, sister, and grandmother could not relieve. Facts are provided about alcoholism, alcoholism is discussed as a disease, and three "Cs," "You didn't cause your parent's drinking; you can't control it; and you can't cure it," are presented. The author further explains that alcoholism can run in families and suggests how to be detached from the disease, how not to place a special burden on the sober parent, and how good intentions can produce bad results. Other chapters include "Letting the Alcoholic Face the Music," "Giving the Alcoholic Loving Support," "When the Parent Gets Sober," and "Changing What You Can." Appendixes cover how to deal with crises related to drunk driving, fire hazards, physical abuse, and where to go for help.

NF

Samz, Jane. **Drugs and Diet.** New York: Chelsea House, 1988. 100p. illus. (The Encyclopedia of Psychoactive Drugs) $17.95. LC 87-30001. ISBN 1-555-462162.

The author of this book cautions that because many Americans do not like the types of foods recommended for most diets, they resort to chemical appetite suppressants to curb their appetites. Chapter titles include "Diet

Drugs," "Prescription Diet Drugs," "Over-the-Counter Diet Pills," "Diuretics: Diet Aid or Diet Danger?," "Laxatives," "Diets," "Eating Disorders," and "Hope for Dieters." The appendix includes a list of state agencies for the prevention and treatment of drug abuse, a bibliography with six items, and a glossary with twenty-six terms.

NF
Sanberg, Paul, and Richard M. T. Krema. **Over-the-Counter Drugs: Harmless or Hazardous.** New York: Chelsea House, 1986. 142p. illus. (The Encyclopedia of Psychoactive Drugs) $17.95. LC 85-17438. ISBN 0-877-54764-5.

The use of psychoactive drugs that are available over-the-counter is examined; the effectiveness and the potential harm each can cause is discussed. Chapters include "The Drugging of America," "Cold Remedies," "Pain Relief," "Stimulants and Diet Aids," "Relief from Anxiety and Insomnia," "Look Alikes," "Placebo," and "Nutritional Supplements." The final chapter asks, "Do I Really Need This?" Appendix includes a list of state agencies for the prevention and treatment of drug abuse, a fifteen-item bibliography, and a glossary of 111 terms.

NF
Sanberg, Paul, and Michael D. Bunsey. **Prescription Narcotics: The Addictive Pain Killers.** New York: Chelsea House, 1986. 104p. illus. (The Encyclopedia of Psychoactive Drugs) $17.95. LC 86-1283. ISBN 0-877-54770-X.

This volume explores the use of prescription narcotics detailing the risks and consequences of addiction. Chapters include "Pain," "The History of the Opiates," "The Effects of Narcotics on the Body," "The Endogenous Opiates," "Prescriptions for Narcotics," "The Treatment of Narcotics Addiction," and "The Challenge Today." The author's preface includes the case of Sue, a Percodan addict and the opiate narcotics used by such historical personages as Elizabeth Barrett Browning, Alexandre Dumas, and Edgar Allen Poe. Current treatments are also described. The appendix includes a list of state agencies for the prevention and treatment of drug abuse, "Further Reading," and a fifty-one-term glossary.

NF
Schlaadt, Richard B., and Peter T. Shannon. **Drugs of Choice: Current Perspectives on Drug Use.** 2d ed. Englewood Cliffs, NJ: Prentice-Hall, Inc., 1986. 320p. illus. charts. diagrams. bibliog. index. $19.95. LC 85-17001. ISBN 0-13-220740-0.

The authors have "attempted to retain the strong points of the first edition and update those areas where changes have occurred." The book places material about drug abuse in perspective and deals with the complexities of drug use in our society. A general overview on drugs currently in use is provided in popularly written fashion. The use of *all* drugs is considered, legal and illicit, although the emphasis is on drugs that are commonly abused. It is pointed out that several legal drugs may be causing as many if not more problems than the illicit drugs that have received considerably more attention.

The book appeals to a wide audience: all those interested in drug education, such as parents, elementary and secondary school teachers, social workers, health professionals, and students. The chapter titles include "Introduction," "Why People Use Drugs," "The Drug Scene," "Pharmacology:

Basic Concepts of Drug Activity," "Stimulants," "Tobacco: America's Number One Preventable Hazard," "Depressants and the Body," "Alcohol: America's Number One Drug Problem," "Opiates," "Hallucinogens," "Marijuana: Still a Controversy," "Over-the-Counter Drugs: What You Can Get Without a Prescription," "Prescription and Other Drugs of Interest," "The Consumer and Drug Legislation," and "Alternatives to Psychoactive Drug Abuse." The book provides a very good, thorough, and unbiased treatment of the subject of substance abuse.

NF
Schlesinger, Stephen E. **Stop Drinking and Start Living**, 2d ed. Blue Ridge Summit, PA: TAB Books, 1989. $7.95. 181p. LC 88-35646. ISBN 0-8306-3227-1.

This book focuses on those who have drinking problems and those who know of someone who has a drinking problem. The authors state that they became more aware of the problem through their clinical work. They realized that many of the people they treated did not have basic information on alcohol or an understanding of their own behavior. The authors feel that one reason more people are coming forth with their drinking problems is that many well-known Americans are exposing their own drinking problems. The book is broken down into four parts: "What Alcohol Does," "What Drinkers Can Do," "What Families and Friends Can Do," and "Resources." The resource section includes "Resource Organizations," "State and Regional Alcoholism Programs," and "State and Highway [safety] Offices."

Reviewed in *Book Report*, January-February 1990.

NF
Schnoll, Sidney H. **Getting Help: Treatments for Drug Abuse.** New York: Chelsea House, 1986. 92p. illus. (The Encyclopedia of Psychoactive Drugs) $17.95. LC 86-1284. ISBN 0-877-54775-0.

Drug abuse is introduced. Information is given on how, when, where, and why people can seek help for drug abuse problems in treatment settings. Acute treatment for intoxication, withdrawal syndromes, and long-term treatment are described. Special treatment populations include pregnant addicts, addicts with psychological disorders, iatrogenic addicts (resulting from unwise medical practice), addicted health professionals, and addicted athletes. Treatment outcomes are reported. Crisis centers, hot lines, self-help groups, and programs in counseling and behavior therapy are described. An appendix includes a list of state agencies for the prevention and treatment of drug abuse, a five-item bibliography, and a thirty-six-term glossary.

NF
Seixas, Judith S. **Drugs: What They Are, What They Do.** New York: Greenwillow, 1987. 47p. illus. (Greenwillow Read-Alone) $10.25. LC 86-33626. ISBN 0-688-07400-6. (GR 5-7)

An easy-to-read, informative book identifying the most common drugs, how they affect you, and why you should say "no" to using them. The illustrations are cartoon-like.

NF

Seixas, Judith S. **Living with a Parent Who Takes Drugs.** New York: Greenwillow Books, 1989. $11.95. LC 89-1995. ISBN 0-688-08627-6. (GR 5-7)

In this story, a seventh-grade boy, Jason, learns to cope with a drug-abusing parent through his school counselor. Alternate courses of action are explained with one being confiding in an adult. Readers learn what drug abuse is, how they can be affected, how addicts are treated, how families may receive help, and the law.

VHS

Sentenced for Life. Los Angeles, CA: Ohlmeyer Communications, 1987. 40 min. video. $29.95. (GR 10-12)

The outcome of drunk driving is shown through a series of case studies of teenage survivors of alcohol-related automobile accidents and the effects on their futures. Separating driving and drinking is set in the context of the cost of being arrested and convicted.

Reviewed in *School Library Journal*, October 1989.

NF

Shader, Laurel. **Drugs and Disease.** New York: Chelsea House, 1987. 111p. illus. (The Encyclopedia of Psychoactive Drugs) $17.95. LC 86-33356. ISBN 1-555-46211-1.

The author states, "One of the legacies of the social upheaval of the 1960s is that psychoactive drugs have become part of the mainstream of American life." He adds, "The U.S. surgeon general estimates that 350,000 people die each year of diseases caused by or exacerbated by cigarette smoking." Pictures of the removel of the bodies of John Belushi and Len Bias bring home the harm that drugs can cause. As the caption under one picture states, "Research has changed perceptions about many drugs once considered harmless. Even nonprescription drugs can have dangerous side effects if they are used improperly or in harmful combinations." Chapter titles include "Tobacco," "Alcohol," "Marijuana," "Cocaine," "Over-the-Counter Medications," and "Drugs and Chronic Disease." The appendix includes a list of state agencies for the prevention and treatment of drug abuse, a six-item reading list, and a glossary with thirty-seven terms.

NF

Shiromoto, Frank N., and Edgar F. Soren. **Drugs and Drinks: Painful Questions, How Substance Abusers and Their Loved Ones Ask for Help.** Lake Bluff, IL: Choices Press, dist. by Quality Books, 1988. 132p. $8.95 pa. LC 88-70397. ISBN 0-9620159-09.

Questions and answers provide information on the various drugs and their effects. Data on the treatment for drug abuse is given and the impact of drug abuse and chemical dependency on families is described. The appendix includes sources for help, tests to determine addiction, a glossary of terms, and a bibliography.

Reviewed in *Booklist*, May 1, 1988.

NF
Siegel, Ronald K. **Intoxication: Life in Pursuit of Artificial Paradise.** New York: Dutton, 1989. 390p. $19.95. LC 88-37411. ISBN 0-525-24764-5.

The author, a research psychopharmacologist, adds the drive for drugs to the drive to satisfy hunger, thirst, and sex. He investigates coffee, alcohol, and drugs, including hallucinogens, opium, marijuana, and cocaine.

Reviewed in *Library Journal*, April 15, 1989.

NF
Silverstein, Alvin, and Virginia B. Silverstein. **Alcoholism.** Philadelphia: J. B. Lippincott Co., 1975. 128p. bibliog. index. $12.89. LC 75-17938. ISBN 0-397-31648-8.

Although this book is intended particularly for young people, it has a wider appeal because it about alcoholism in general. The material is presented in an objective manner and is surprisingly pleasant to read. Major aspects of alcohol use and abuse are discussed.

The following chapters are included: "The Number One Problem," "Alcoholic Beverages," "What Alcohol Does in the Body," "Alcohol in History," "Drinking Today—Social Drinking and Problem Drinking," "Drinking and Driving," "Teenage Drinking," "What Is Alcoholism," "Treating the Alcoholic," "Living with an Alcoholic Parent," "A Personal Decision," and "For Further Information."

VHS
Smoking: Everything You and Your Family Need to Know. Producer: John Mernit for Home Box Office. New York: Ambrose Video Publishing, 1989. 30 min. video. $99.95. (GR 8-12)

The response of U.S. Surgeon General C. Everett Koop to questions about smoking. Statistics and research information are presented to support an antismoking program. A brief segment of a patient dying from lung cancer highlights the message that smoking is not only dangerous, but can be fatal. To move the video from the "talking head" format, ads and interviews are interspersed.

Reviewed in *Booklist*, July 1989.

FLM/VHS
Smokeless Tobacco: It Can Snuff You Out. Los Angeles, CA: Alfred Higgins, 1986. 13 min. film, $295.00; video, $265.00.

Smokeless tobacco, most often seen in the mouths of popular athletes, is thought of by the uninformed as a safe substitute for smoking. This video presents the dangers of use, the increase in oral cancer, and the problems in the area of dental hygiene. The point is made that it is no easier to quit the use of smokeless tobacco than it is to stop smoking.

Reviewed in *Library Journal*, November 15, 1986.

FIC
Snyder, Anne. **First Step.** New York: NAL, 1976. 132p. $2.95. LC 75-4867. ISBN 0-0301-4651-8.

In this story, a tormented high school girl gradually resolves the problems brought on by an alcoholic mother and conflict over responsibility to the family. The girl is finally introduced to Alateen, although at first she resists the program. The book does not promise that alcoholism and the attendant family problems are easily cured, but it shows that the first step involves acceptance, compassion, and personal strength, all of which can lessen the control a parent's alcoholism inflicts on children's lives.

FIC

Snyder, Anne. **My Name Is Davy—I'm an Alcoholic**. New York: NAL, 1978. 144p. $2.50. LC 76-28457. ISBN 0-451-14976-9 pa.

Suitable for teenagers, this is a story about two alcoholic high school students. The girl realizes they need help, but the boy won't believe he is an alcoholic and only halfheartedly agrees to seek the help of Alcoholics Anonymous. The boy's anger and disdain for the attempt to quit are responsible for the girl's death. Overcome with guilt, the boy goes on a rampage and finally ends up at Alcohlics Anonymous facing reality. It is a sensational story with a clear message.

NF

Sonnett, Sherry. **Smoking.** New York: Watts, 1988. 72p. diagrams. illus. bibliog. index. $9.90. LC 87-16482. ISBN 0-531-10489-3. (GR 6-10)

This book contains information on the history of smoking, its effects on the health of various organs, its immediate and long-term health hazards, the dangers of passive smoking, and the risks to pregnant smokers. It is well illustrated with photographs, cartoons, and charts.

VHS

Speak Up, Speak Out: Learning to Say No to Drugs. Mount Kisco, NY: Guidance Associates, 1988. (Drug Free Schools Videos) 15 min. video. $59.00. (GR 9-12)

Another entry in the "How to Say 'No' to Drugs" trend. Teenagers are given ways to say no to drugs and alcohol. The scenario is the senior trip to Washington and the protagonists are two males. Steve convinces his friend, Matt, to have an alcohol and possibly drug party in Matt's own hotel room. Many of the other seniors try to help Matt say no, but it is only when he realizes that Steve is setting him up to take the heat for any unfortunate outcomes that Matt is able to say it. Teachers' guide is included.

NF

Spence, Annette. **Substance Abuse.** New York: Facts on File, 1989. 128p. (Encyclopedia of Good Health Series) $16.95. LC 87-21142. ISBN 0-8160-1669-0. (GR 5-10)

Information on tobacco, alcohol, and drugs is presented from both a medical and a social point of view. Including a historical perspective, the question-and-answer format features simple questions that reflect the junior high-age student. The answers are well supported with statistics. The appendix includes further sources of information, a list of organizations, and a glossary.

Reviewed in *Book Report*, November-December 1989.

VHS
Staying Off Cocaine: Avoiding Relapse. Producer: Reelizations. Pleasantville, NY: Human Relations Media, 1988. 38 min. video. $225.00. (GR 9-12)

This video is directed toward counselors who work with recovering cocaine users and the users themselves. This is more useful to rehabilitation centers than to home or classroom use. The presentation is positive and takes into consideration many possible setbacks of recovering drug users.

Reviewed in *School Library Journal*, May 1989.

NF
Stepney, Rob. **Alcohol.** New York: Watts, 1987. 64p. (Understanding Drugs Series) $11.90. LC 87-50597. ISBN 0-531-10433-8. (GR 6-9)

The nature, origins, and effects of alcohol on the user are described with additional information on the production of alcohol. Alcohol use and abuse are discussed and there are photographs demonstrating the physical and mental health detriments. A summary fact file and a listing of sources for help are included.

Reviewed in *Booklist*, January 1, 1988, and *School Library Journal*, March 1988.

NF
Stepney, Rob. **Tobacco.** New York: Watts, 1987. 62p. LC 87-50596. ISBN 0-531-10438-9. (GR 4-9)

The author declares tobacco to be the most damaging of drugs. Diseases resulting from tobacco use and the hazards of second-hand smoking are graphically displayed.

Reviewed in *Booklist*, January 1, 1988, and *School Library Journal*, March 1988.

VHS
The Steroid Trap: Turning Winners Into Losers. Mount Kisco, NY: Guidance Associates, 1990. 40 min. video. $219.00.

This video explores who uses steroids, and why and how steroids work. The adverse effects of taking steroids are explained. A coach, students, and the guidance counselor discuss the desire to appear to be larger, stronger, and taller as it relates to self-esteem. Athletes discuss their steroid use and individuals talk about their increased aggression, mood swings, changes in sex characteristics, psychotic symptoms, and the possibility of liver cancer.

VHS
Steroids: Crossing the Line. Princeton, NJ: Films for the Humanities, 1988. 1989 release. 54 min. video. $149.00. (GR 10-12)

A former Olympic athlete who was a user, under a doctor's care, for steroids is the focal point for a discussion of legal, ethical, and medical concerns. One real line this athlete crossed was the international boundary between Mexico and the U.S. His arrest for smuggling brings up the legal aspects. The medical effects are illustrated by a death attributed to steroids and by the physical and mental changes described in interviews with experts, users, and ex-users. Jenkins considers that drug testing will be ineffective and that athletes must be educated concerning the dangers. While the ethical questions are asked throughout, one of the most important comes when athletes continue to use steroids even when they understand the side effects.

Reviewed in *School Library Journal*, February 1989.

VHS
Steroids: Shortcut to Make-Believe Muscles. Northbrook, IL: Film Ideas, 1988. 35 min. video. $125.00. (Available in both ½" and ¾") (GR 8-12)

This two-part video explains that anabolic steroids are a risky shortcut to muscle-building. Factual information is given about steroids, including what they are, harmful effects of long-term usage, medical uses, how to say no, and the many side effects. The second part of the video demonstrates how to plan and execute a drug-free body development program using dumbbell fly, bicep/tricep exercises, and specific exercises for women, among others. In this way muscular bodies can be developed without using steroids. Good nutrition is also considered a healthy alternative.

Reviewed in *Booklist*, June 1988.

VHS
Stop Before You Drop. Producer: I. W. Harper. Washington, D.C.: Durrin Productions, 1988; released 1989. 12 min. video. $205.00.

Music is used to help young adults resist peer pressure and advertising to smoke. Some suggestions are given on how to quit.

Reviewed in *Booklist*, January 1, 1990.

FIC
Strasser, Todd. **The Accident.** New York: Delacorte, 1988. 178p. $14.95. LC 87-36411. ISBN 0-440-50061-3. (GR 6-9)

A fatal accident kills four teenagers who have been to a beer party. The hero, eighteen-year-old Matt, is concerned that the police investigation is a cover-up hiding the identity of the person who was responsible for the accident.

FIC
Strasser, Todd. **Angel Dust Blues.** New York: Putnam, 1981. 203p. $9.95. LC 78-31735. ISBN 0-698-20485-9.

This is a novel, the story of a high school student, Alex, who becomes increasingly alienated from his successful parents. They spend the winter in Florida while their son remains in the family home near New York with a housekeeper. Alex becomes involved with drug dealing through friends. The trouble get deeper and deeper, and the only bright spot in Alex's life is a new girlfriend who helps him to see that he must accept responsibilities.

Eventually, Alex is faced with a hard decision where a fugitive drug-dealing friend is concerned. Alex decides to turn him in because he feels the friend must have medical assistance. It is the right choice, although the friend will perhaps die of an overdose of drugs anyway. Alex realizes at last that he will be able to act on his own and make the correct decisions no matter what the relationship with his parents and others is. It is a touching story, well told, and with a viewpoint that may help young people.

NF
Strom-Paikin, Joyce E. **Medical Treason: Nurses on Drugs.** Far Hills, NJ: New Horizon Press, 1989. 311p. $21.95. LC 89-60104. ISBN 0-88282-043-5.

This is an autobiographical account of a young nurse who became involved in the drug trade in her own hospital. When she recognized that drug trading was going on, she volunteered to gather evidence against the hospital staff involved, acting as an undercover agent for the police. The incident made her decide to leave hospital nursing and become a psychiatric nurse clinician.

Reviewed in *Library Journal*, July 1989.

FLM/VHS
Struggle Within. Producer: Clip/Buffalo Cherokee Productions. Van Nuys, CA: AIMS Media, 1989. 16 min. film, $395.00; video, $325.00. (GR 7-12)

The "hero," Bobby, has a drunk driving accident and ruins his friend Charlie's knee and, consequently, his hopes for a football career. Bobby continues to drink to escape his feelings of guilt and the loss of his girlfriend until Charlie comes to see him. Finally, Bobby acknowledges his need for help.

Reviewed in *School Library Journal*, December 1989.

NF
Stwertka, Eve, and Albert Stwertka. **Marijuana.** New York: Watts, 1986. 64p. $9.40. LC 85-22526. ISBN 0-531-0122-3. (GR 5-9)

These authors have revised an earlier edition to present a general history of marijuana use, including its history, source, cultivation, chemistry, ways of consumption, side effects, and continuing popularity. Facts about the medical use of marijuana, statistics, research, and attitudes are presented to allow readers to make their own decisions. The debate over legalization is also presented. A glossary of terms is provided, and black-and-white photographs illustrate the text. A list of names and addresses of organizations who offer help has been provided.

Reviewed in *Booklist*, March 1987; and *School Library Journal*, March 1987.

NF
Taylor, Barbara. **Everything You Need to Know about Alcohol.** New York: Rosen Publishing Group, 1989. 64p. index. glossary. bibliog. illus. $12.95. LC 88-39820. ISBN 0-8239-0813-5.

The effects of alcohol on mind and body are described in this very easy-to-read, large-print book. Chapter titles include "What Is Alcohol?," "Attitudes Towards Alcohol," "Alcohol Users: Adults and Teenagers," "The Effects of Alcohol on the Human Body," "Alcoholism: What Is It?," "The Treatment of Alcoholism," and "Alcohol and You." Pictures, some in color, and diagrams illustrate the text. The book closes with a glossary of twenty-eight terms, a list of places for persons in jeopardy from alcohol abuse or drunk driving problems "to go for help," and a list of eight titles "for further reading."

NF

Taylor, L. B. **Driving High: The Hazards of Driving, Drinking and Drugs.** New York: Watts, 1983. 120p. index. illus. (An Impact Book) $12.90. LC 83-6821. ISBN 0-531-04663-X. (GR 7-10)

The hazards of driving high from drinking or drug use are detailed, beginning with a scenario of a fatal automobile accident. Statistics are presented with an analysis of the reasons teenagers drink. The effects of alcohol and marijuana on the body are detailed. Suggestions are made for teenagers interested in becoming active in solving the drunk-driver problem. A bibliography and sources for additional information are provided.

Reviewed in *Booklist*, November 1, 1983.

NF

Theodore, Alan. **The Origins and Sources of Drugs.** New York: Chelsea House, 1988. 121p. illus. (The Encyclopedia of Psychoactive Drugs) $17.95. LC 87-35233. ISBN 1-555-46234-0.

This book presents the history, source, and nature of both legal and illicit drugs. Black-and-white pictures ably illustrate this book. Chapter titles include "Cocaine," "Products of the Indian Hemp Plant," "Products of the Poppy: Opium, Morphine, and Heroin," "Alcohol," "Nicotine," "Caffeine," and "Hallucinogenic Drugs from Plants." The appendix includes a list of state agencies for the prevention and treatment of drug abuse, a bibliography with nine citations, and a glossary with thirty-three terms.

VHS

Tough Questions—Straight Answers. Producer and director: Bob Larsen. New York: Star Classics, 1987, released 1989. 90 min. video. $34.95. (GR 7)

Everyday events such as wanting the car provide a father with the opportunity to talk over a variety of ticklish topics such as peer pressure and substance abuse. Health professionals confirm and explain further the facts presented after each segment.

Reviewed in *Booklist*, December 15, 1989.

NF

Trager, Oliver, ed. **Drugs in America: Crisis or Hysteria?** Facts on File, 1986. 190p. (An Editorials on File Book) illus. index. $24.95. LC 87-6812. ISBN 0-81601775-1.

The preface of this volume states, "But while drug abuse has undoubtedly resulted in many personal tragedies throughout the country, its importance as a problem may be exaggerated by politicians all too eager to appease a concerned public...." This collection of editorials on the use and abuse of drugs and the treatment of that topic by law enforcement and the legal system is designed to explore "the U.S. government's and the American public's often contradictory attitude concerning this thorny issue through the words and images of America's leading editorial writers and cartoonists." Part I includes "Schedule I Substances (Marijuana, Heroin, Cocaine)." Articles are reproduced on the death of comedian John Belushi, from the *Oklahoma City Times, The Detroit News*, and others. Part II is "Law Enforcement & the Reagan Administration's Drug Wars"; part III includes "Smuggling"; and part IV is "Education, Schools, and Teenagers." Part V features "Drugs in Sports."

NF

Trulson, Michael E. **LSD: Visions or Nightmares.** New York: Chelsea House, 1985. 128p. illus. (The Encyclopedia of Psychoactive Drugs) $17.95. LC 84-14936. ISBN 0-877-54752-1.

Lysergic acid diethylamide (LSD) provides visions and nightmares. Chapter titles include "Discovery and Uses of LSD," "Hallucinogens: What They Are," "Effects of LSD," "The LSD Experience," "Flashbacks," "Toxic Effects of LSD," "Therapy for Abusers of LSD," and "Hallucinogens and the Animal Kingdom." The appendix includes "Helping a Friend with an LSD Problem," "Case Studies," "Reactions to LSD," a list of state agencies for the prevention and treatment of drug abuse, and a glossary with sixty-eight terms.

VHS

Trying to Find Normal. Hospital Satellite Network. Distributed by: AIMS Media, Van Nuys, CA, 1988. 17 min. video. $325.00. (GR 9-adult)

A companion to *Adult Children of Alcoholics* and *Alcohol, Children, and the Family*, this film tells the story of a thirty-year-old artist dealing with his childhood in a home characterized by alcohol abuse. The problems generated for adults who were children in alcoholic homes is presented.

Reviewed in *School Library Journal*, July 1989.

NF

Twerski, Abraham J. **Caution: "Kindness" Can Be Dangerous to the Alcoholic.** Englewood Cliffs, NJ: Prentice-Hall, 1981. 174p. bibliog. index. (A Spectrum Book) $9.95; $4.95 pa. LC 81-605. ISBN 0-13-121244-3; 0-13-121236-2 pa.

Dr. Twerski's book can be profitably read by anyone interested in treating the alcoholic, including friends, family members, physicians, and alcoholism counselors. The physician describes "the enabler" or "alcoholism accomplice," a person who behaves in such a way as to help the alcoholic avoid the unpleasant consequences of his drinking problem, thereby allowing him to continue his self-destructive drinking. The enabler ordinarily wants to help, but this help most often takes the form of lethal benevolent behavior.

The book cites examples of lethal benevolent behavior, such as a lawyer father who used his influence to have drunken-driving charges against his son dropped. Twerski thinks society's attitude in general toward drunken drivers is lethal benevolence. He says, "The combination of legal niceties, long delays before trial, plea bargaining, and misguided sympathy adds up to a system that allows the carnage to run rampant." All this in spite of how we preach against drunken driving.

Twerski's solution to the alcoholism problem includes the use of Alcoholics Anonymous and similar resources, honest confrontation, no cushioning of the alcoholic, and breaking down the alcoholic's denial of the problem and facing it. He says if this doesn't work, and there is a crisis, there will be only about a 50 percent chance of mortality, whereas not confronting carries about a 100 percent chance of mortality.

FLM/VHS

Under the Influence 2: A Decade Later. Producer: R. Randall Frederick and Yvonne Parsons. Director: Tim Armstrong. Santa Barbara, CA: FMS Productions, 1988. 27 min. film, $550.00; video, $495.00. (GR 9-12)

The relationship between substance abuse and driving skills is graphically demonstrated by showing the effect of alcohol and drugs on cadets at the California Highway Patrol Academy. Diminishing judgment, coordination, and vision appear to startle the cadets and should inform the audience.

Reviewed in *Booklist*, August 1988.

NF

U.S. Department of Education, Office of Educational and Improvement Research. **Drug Prevention Curricula: A Guide to Selection and Implementation.** National Clearinghouse for Alcohol and Drug Information, Box 2345, Rockville, MD 20852. 65p. free.

This publication is a response to requests for assistance in the choice of substance abuse prevention curricula. It includes goals of a good K-12 curriculum, instructional approaches for different grade levels, and suggestions for involving parents and the community in choosing, implementing, and supporting the curriculum. Ways to reach high-risk populations and children in special education classes are suggested. Staff training is outlined and the means for evaluating K-12 prevention curriculum and the comprehensive program of which it is a part is detailed. Finally important resources for assistance and information are listed.

NF

Wadler, Gary I. **Drugs and the Athlete.** Philadelphia: F. A. Davis, 1989. 353p. bibliog. index. $19.95. LC 88-33612. ISBN 0-8036-9008-8.

The use of anabolic steroids, cocaine, and diuretics by athletes is presented with the reasons that athletes use both legal and illegal drugs. Each drug is explained, beginning with a history of the drug, its chemistry and physiology, the clinical pharmacology, use in sports, and, finally, the diverse effects. Methods for detecting drug abuse and legal considerations are covered. Chapters are well documented with bibliographies, and the appendix includes drug policies and position statements of various sports associations.

Reviewed in *Library Journal*, July 1989.

NF

Wall, Robert T. **Standing Tall Above Drugs: A Modern Crusade.** Muncie, IN: Accelerated Development, Inc., 1989. 333p. $19.95. LC 88-70587. ISBN 0-915202-82-4.

This book is divided into three parts, "Alpha ... The Beginning," "Beckoning ... Growth Options," and "Commitment ... A Synergistic Path." Within part I, the chapters read, "Rising Above the Crowd," "No Is Not Enough," "Check Under the Hood, Please," and "Living on the Edge." The chapter "No Is Not Enough" includes one section on "We've Got Your Number," an introduction to numerology. Part II includes "The Kindred Spirit," "Sesame Street Revisited," "Signs of the Times," and "Getting to the Heart of the Matter." Part III discusses "Breaking Into the Perfect Circle," "Capture the Moment," "Stretching the Process," and "Star Spangled Spirit." The author drifts from the major theme with asides such as "The 120-Year Old

Man," a section presenting information on a probable national average life-span of 120 years. He comments, "People are literally working, drinking, smoking, and drugging themselves to death. If they don't die on the job, many suffer the accumulation of work-related distress and lead a morose existence in retirement." This book is included for that special audience who would welcome tests of synergy and suggestions for improving management techniques as well as ways to overcome drug abuse through assessment of motivation and basic values.

NF

Ward, Brian. **Smoking and Health.** New York: Watts, 1986. 48p. $10.90. LC 85-52043. ISBN 0-531-10180-0. (GR 5-up)

Large print and colorful pictures make this book more appealing to the student with fewer reading skills. Chapter titles include "Smoking as an Addiction," "How Tobacco Smoke Affects the Body," "Smoking and the Lungs," "Smoking and the Heart," "The Introduction of Tobacco," "The Spread of the Smoking Habit," "Tobacco Cultivation and Processing," "Tobacco in All Its Forms," "The Cost to the Community," "Breathing Other People's Smoke," "Tobacco and the Child," "The Special Risks for Women," "Giving Up," "Changing Attitudes," "The Right to Choose," and "The Moral Problem." The glossary has nineteen terms.

NF

Washton, Arnold M., and Donna Boundy. **Cocaine and Crack: What You Need to Know.** Hillside, NJ: Enslow, 1989. 95p. diagrams. photos. illus. bibliog. index. $13.95. LC 88-16814. ISBN 0-89490-162-1. (GR 6-8)

In an effort to discourage children from experimenting with drugs, the dangers of crack and cocaine are described, including the possibility of taking an overdose on .an amount previously tolerated. The emphasis is on the biological basis of drug dependency. Chapters include "An Epidemic of Cocaine Use," "Some Basic Facts," "Dangerous Myths," "A Powerful Addiction," "Who Gets Addicted?," "Cocaine's Other Risks," "If Someone You Care About Has a Cocaine Problem," and "Prevention." The drug is presented in its various forms and the affect on the physiology is detailed so that the reader will understand why it is so habit-forming. The presentation of cocaine shows that even casual use is highly risky. The historical perspective is given as well as the ways cocaine affects the economy, employees in the workplace, and society. Illustrations are black-and-white photographs. The glossary has fifty-nine items; the bibliography has nine books and ten periodical articles.

Reviewed in *Booklist*, April 1, 1989; *School Library Journal*, May 1989.

NF

Wassmer, Arthur. **Recovering Together: How To Help an Alcoholic without Hurting Yourself.** New York: St. Martin's, 1989. 256p. $16.95. LC 89-35075. ISBN 0-312-03416-4.

The author, a clinical psychologist, is a specialist in addictive disorders. Writing from personal experience, he presents the concepts of codependency and alcohol as diseases with brief examples from the lives of his patients. These short case studies outline the effect of alcoholism on family and friends and explain the need for addict and codependent to recover together. Sources of help are provided, along with guidelines for evaluating individuals and organizations that help alcoholics and their families.

Reviewed in *Library Journal*, November 1, 1989.

VHS
Weigh the Cost: The Prevention of Adolescent Alcohol Use through Decision Making. Producer: Farnsworth Communications. Northbrook, IL: Film Ideas, 1988. 27 min. video. $110.00. (GR 7-11)

This video is about John, who is pressured to join his friends in a drinking party. He is helped in making his decision by talking with friends and also by dreaming he is on trial weighing the alternatives. John goes through a six-step rational process. "The steps, applicable to most problems, here are focused on drinking.... They include: defining the problem, gathering information, determining alternatives, examining feelings, making and evaluating the decision." Questions relating to John's problem, his behavior, and the viewer's opinion appear on the screen after each step. It is recommended that the video should be stopped at these points to encourage discussion.

Reviewed in *School Library Journal*, October 1989.

NF
Weisberg, Jeffrey, and Gene Hawes. **Rx for Recovery: The Medical and Health Guide for Alcoholics, Addicts and Their Families.** New York: Watts, 1989. 345p. $19.95. LC 88-51593. ISBN 0-531-15096-8. (GR 10-adult)

One of the authors of this volume is a physician who has worked with both addicts and alcoholics. Although the book is written for adults, high school students can use the information provided. The "adult" designation describes the smaller print and longer, less familiar words, rather than the content. Chapter titles include "Reaching for Recovery: A Medical Perspective," "How Family Members Can Help an Alcoholic or Addict in the Family—and Greatly Help Themselves," "How to Choose and Work with Doctors," "Building Good Health in Recovery from Alcoholism/Addiction," "Avoiding Special Hazards with Common Health Problems," "Avoiding Special Hazards with Medicines," "Women in Recovery and Their Special Needs," "Dealing with Associated Diseases," "Dealing with Mental Illness," and "Dealing with Chronic Illness." The appendixes include "Directory of Sources of Help and Further Information" and "Directory of Leading Treatment Centers for Alcoholism/Addiction in the United States and Canada" (listed by state or province). Information on each treatment center includes the name of the director, capacity, types of patients admitted, the inpatient treatment program, outpatient treatment program, family programs or services, charges for treatment, health-care insurance regulations, accreditation agencies, aftercare programs, recovery rates and a very brief "comments."

Reviewed in *Library Journal*, April 15, 1989.

FLM/VHS
When Your Parent Drinks Too Much. Producer and director: Jerry Haislmaier. Deerfield, IL: MTI Film and Video, 1987. 27 min. guide. film, $575.00; video, $250.00. (GR 6-11)

Based on Ryerson's book (see under author) teenagers discuss their experiences in their homes with alcoholic parent(s). The major messages are that they did not cause the problem and that they cannot control or cure abuse.

Reviewed in *Booklist*, September 1, 1988.

NF
Wholey, Dennis. **Becoming Your Own Parent: The Solution for Adult Children of Alcoholic and Other Dysfunctional Families**. New York: Doubleday, 1988. 312p. $17.95. LC 88-9710. ISBN 0-385-24591-2. (Adult)

Having experienced alcoholism in his own family, this author presents the case studies of fourteen individuals who tell about their progress from "abysmal dysfunctioning to recovery." From childhood through adulthood, the impact of alcoholism, overeating, gambling, workaholics, and chemical dependency is described. Solutions are offered to the problems, and the interviews discuss how recovery is possible.

Reviewed in *Booklist*, October 15, 1988.

NF
Williams, Terry. **The Cocaine Kids: The Inside Story of a Teenage Drug Ring.** Reading, MA: Addison-Wesley, 1989. 160p. $16.95. LC 89-6505. ISBN 0-201-09360-X.

The author, a sociologist, followed the activities of a teenage cocaine ring in New York's Spanish Harlem from 1982 to 1986. Gaining the confidence of several, he was allowed to become a part of this world, observing their business operations. A glossary is provided to help understand the vocabulary, for the story is told in street language. A graphic picture is presented of the adulterating of cocaine, and the packaging, selling, and usage. The author has also given information concerning what has happened to Charlie, Chillie, Hector, Jake, Kitty, Masterrap, and Splib since 1986. Since the book is nonjudgmental, some readers may not notice the violence and danger in this world.

Reviewed in *Booklist*, August 1989; *Library Journal*, July 1989.

NF
Winger, Gail. **Valium: The Tranquil Trap.** New York: Chelsea House, 1986. 119p. illus. (The Encyclopedia of Psychoactive Drugs) $17.95. LC 86-1282. ISBN 0-877-54759-9.

This volume examines the nature, effects, and dangers of the use and abuse of valium and other related anti-anxiety drugs. Chapter titles include "Anxiety and the Minor Tranquilizers," "Beyond Anxiety: The Many Uses of Benzodiazepines," "How Dangerous Are the Minor Tranquilizers?," "Patterns of Tranquilizer Use," "Coping With Anxiety: Tranquilizers and Their Alternatives," and "Economic Issues and Prescribing Practices." The appendix includes "How to Tell If Someone Has a Valium Problem," "Rules for Safer Use of Valium," a listing of state agencies for the prevention and treatment of drug abuse, and a glossary with fifty-seven terms.

NF
Woods, Geraldine, and Harold Woods. **Cocaine.** New York: Watts, 1985. illus. (A First Book) $10.40. LC 85-15523. ISBN 0-531-10035-9. (GR 5-8)

This study of the effects and abuse of cocaine includes a history of its use and trade. A discussion is included of the treatments for cocaine addiction.

NF
Woods, Geraldine. **Drug Use and Drug Abuse.** New York: Watts, 1986. 2d ed., rev. 64p. illus. (A First Book) $9.90. LC 85-22531. ISBN 0-531-10114-2 (GR 5-8)

A simply written book with colorful illustrations, this introduction to drug use and drug abuse could be useful to the high school student with a reading problem.

NF
Young, Patrick. **Drugs and Pregnancy.** New York: Chelsea House, 1987. 108p. illus. (The Encyclopedia of Psychoactive Drugs) $17.95. LC 86-24492. ISBN 1-555-46203-0.

The risks of taking drugs, both legal and illicit, during pregnancy are examined. Chapter titles include "Pregnancy," "Drugs and the Body," "Alcohol," "Smoking," "Drugs of Abuse," "Medications," and "Breast Feeding." The appendix includes a list of state agencies for the prevention and treatment of drug abuse and a glossary of fifty-six terms.

NF
Young, Patrick. **Mental Disturbances.** New York: Chelsea House, 1988. 166p. illus. (The Encyclopedia of Psychoactive Drugs) $17.95. LC 87-25688. ISBN 1-555-46206-5.

The varied types of mental illnesses are described. Their symptoms and treatment are discussed as well as the reactions that certain drugs induce that closely resemble mental illness. Chapter titles include "Depression and Mania," "Schizophrenia," "Anxiety, Panic Attacks, and Agoraphobia," "Simple and Social Phobias," "Obsessive-Compulsive Behavior," "Anorexia Nervosa and Bulimia," and "Hysteria." The appendix includes the name of the phobia and the fear associated with it, state agencies for the prevention and treatment of drug abuse, and a glossary of fifty-one terms.

NF
Zackon, Fred. **Heroin: The Street Narcotic.** New York: Chelsea House, 1986. 136p. illus. (The Encyclopedia of Psychoactive Drugs) $17.95. LC 85-31440. ISBN 0-877-547696.

This volume examines the history, characteristics, and dangers of heroin use. Chapters include "Poppies and Population: A Brief History," "Heroin Addiction in the Modern World," "How Heroin Affects Its Users," "Theories of Heroin Addiction," "The Challenge of Recovery," and "Treatment and Rehabilitation." Opium was used as early as 5,000 years ago in ancient Mesopotamia. The book discusses growth of use, the ability of users to become tolerant to the effects of the drug, and the rehabilitation treatment associated with heroin. Three portraits of heroin users are included. The appendix includes a list of state agencies for the prevention and treatment of drug abuse, five citations for further reading, and a glossary of forty-four terms.

2

Reference Works

This chapter lists a variety of nonfiction materials including periodicals that are defined by the authors as references. We consider "reference works" to be sources such as bibliographies, dictionaries, glossaries, or encyclopedias that would be used for instant information rather than data or text for more in-depth analysis. Emphasis has also been placed on information found in machine-readable format. Materials have been divided into books and databases.

Many publishers are providing their reference tools on CD-ROM as well as hard copy. As this and similar technologies proliferate, it becomes necessary to expand secondary school collections to include these additional sources of information in school library media centers. The required equipment and spaces within the facility quickly become evident and the need to plan for these new formats is immediate. The numbers of materials that can be found *only* in machine-readable format now will increase in the immediate future, making it even more critical that librarians and school library media specialists plan for automation and new technologies in all public libraries and school library media centers.

Periodicals have been included that deal directly with substance abuse. It is assumed that public librarians and school library media specialists will direct their clientele to the materials on substance abuse found in general periodicals and newspapers by searching *Magazine Index, Readers' Guide to Periodical Literature, Education Index*, and *Newsbank* among others. For the reader of this volume who is unfamiliar with possible search terminology, a suggested list of subject headings to begin searching may be found in the introduction to this volume or in the list of Library of Congress headings in Appendix B. Further a sample search on BRS is included in Appendix C.

BOOKS

Abel, Ernest L., comp. **A Comprehensive Guide to the Cannabis Literature.** Westport, CT: Greenwood Press, 1979. 699p. index. $56.95. LC 78-20014. ISBN 0-313-32721-6.

While the literature covered in this bibliography was published before 1978, it provides a reference to the past literature and is still in print. It deals with the marijuana plant *Cannabis sativa L* in virtually all of its aspects: psychotomimetic properties, industrial usage, cultivation, history, and legal status. The coverage is quite comprehensive, including materials from both popular and scholarly books and periodicals. In addition, some foreign-language citations have been included, translated into English. No items from newspapers and newsletters have been listed.

The 8,177 entries are arranged alphabetically by senior author in one sequence, except for a supplementary addendum containing unintentionally omitted items and those published after the main bibliography was compiled. The latter is arranged in a separate alphabetical sequence. The compiler has supplied an introductory essay of about twenty pages which covers historical background, chemistry, analysis, pharmacology, physiological effects, therapeutic uses, prevalence, behavioral effects, and psychiatric considerations. A list of abbreviations of journals cited has been provided.

There are no annotations. Although there is a subject index, there is no access by author except through the senior author. A limited spot check of a few entries showed an unusually high number of errors in references.

Abel, Ernest L., comp. **Drugs and Sex: A Bibliography.** Westport, CT: Greenwood Press, 1983. 129p. index. $36.95. LC 83-5656. ISBN 0-313-23941-X.

Abel is a research scientist who has prepared several bibliographies on topics related to drug abuse. This work treats a topic of perpetual interest, substances that may have an effect on sex drive or performance. The consensus of opinion currently is that there is no such thing as an aphrodisiac. On the other hand, the rise of the drug culture has increased interest in investigating substances that may have a negative impact on sexuality, normal performance, or the physiology of sex. There is also interest in scrutinizing certain substances that are used to treat nonsexual problems because they may have side effects that cause sexual dysfunction.

Abel's rather comprehensive bibliography begins with an essay which defines some of the technical terms he uses, discusses mechanisms of action of drugs, and individually treats alcohol, amphetamines, antidepressants, barbiturates, benzodiazepines, caffeine, cocaine, LSD, marijuana, methaqualone, narcotics, nitrites, phencyclidine, and tobacco. The 1,432 references are then listed alphabetically by author under these headings plus "Antipsychotics" and "General Reviews." There is a subject index only; to find an individual author's work one must search through each section.

The bibliography makes an important contribution because there are no other extensive lists on this subject, and the general public as well as researchers are interested in it.

Abel, Ernest L. **A Marihuana Dictionary: Words, Terms, Events, and Persons Relating to Cannabis.** Westport, CT: Greenwood Press, 1982. 136p. bibliog. index. $36.95. LC 81-134427. ISBN 0-313-23252-0.

Marijuana was introduced to Americans about 1900 by Mexican workers who carried it across the border. Before then the plant was known as hemp in the U.S. and was valued only as a source of fiber for rope and twine. By the 1960s, use of the plant as a drug of abuse had spread to middle class young Americans, although it was and still is illegal. Marijuana users have developed a special lingo or argot as a means of fostering group solidarity. The compiler of this dictionary points out that like all slang, marijuana lingo is constantly changing. A core of terms has remained, though, and that is the main subject matter of this compilation.

Abel has provided a rather comprehensive list of words and phrases. Their derivation is included when known with citations to earliest use in popular media. Also included are terms referring to hemp that were once used but are now obsolete. Individuals concerned with the history of marijuana are listed, as are events related to the subject. Terms related to the pharmacological and botanical properties of the plan are also included. A short appendix of foreign-language terms is provided. The bibliography lists sources referred to in the definitions. Abel is well qualified to write a dictionary such as this, and it is an interesting and valuable contribution to the literature of drug abuse.

Alcoholism and Drug Abuse Treatment Centers Directory: A Guide to Alcoholism and Drug Abuse Treatment Centers and Services. Santa Monica, CA: Ready Reference, 1981. 350p. $47.50 pa. LC 80-25164. ISBN 0-916270-25-4.

Listed in this directory are more than 9,000 federal, state, and local treatment centers. The directory is arranged alphabetically by state and then subdivided by city. The address of each center is provided with phone number and a statement about whether it is a drug or alcohol unit or both. In addition to the state listings, there are also special listings for Puerto Rico and the U.S. territories, Veterans Administration medical centers, and a list of official state authorities.

Because of the increasing number of alcohol and drug abusers requiring help, there is a need to be able to refer individuals to proper treatment facilities. This work seems to be up-to-date and accurate, and it is conveniently arranged for quick reference use.

The American Society of Hospital Pharmacists. **New Consumer Drug Digest.** New York: Facts on File, 1985. 528p. index. $10.95 pa. LC 81-12499. ISBN 0-8160-1254-7; ISBN 0-8160-1255-5 pa.

The introduction provides very brief essays on how drugs act, dosage forms and methods of administration, toxicity, teratogenicity, how drugs reach the market, over-the-counter and prescription drugs, and expenditures for drugs. Drugs are listed under the following chapter headings, "Heart Diseases and Diseases of the Circulatory System," "Infections," "Skin Problems," "Asthma and Other Breathing Problems," "Stomach and Intestinal Problems," "Allergies, Colds, and Coughs," "Arthritis," "Pain," "Diabetes," "Glaucoma," "Seizures and Epilepsy," "Gout," "Parkinson's Disease," "Thyroid Disease," "Sleep Disturbances," "Psychiatric Problems," and "Miscellaneous Drugs." Each drug is listed by its generic name followed by the correct pronunciation. The brand names are then given with the uses, the undesired effects, precautions, dosage, and storage. The appendix contains a list of Canadian brand names.

Anderson, Kenneth, and Lois Anderson. **Orphan Drugs.** Los Angeles, CA: Body Press, 1988. 253p. bibliog. index. $14.95 pa. LC 87-35933. ISBN 9-89586-643-9.

This volume contains 1,500 generic and brand-name drugs in an alphabetical list by generic name. When the generic name is not known, the entry may be traced through a symptoms directory that is difficult to use. For each entry, the brand names are given as well as the actions of the drug, the disorders the drug may cure, precautions for using the drug, the dosage, the present manufacturer, and the country of manufacture. These are drugs that have been tested or licensed in countries outside of the United States, but, because they lack Federal Drug Administration approval, they are not available here. Some have yet to be patented while others have not been chosen by a manufacturer in the U.S. The addresses of the 200 manufacturers are arranged in alphabetical order in a separate directory. The author of this book is a former editor of *Today's Health.*

Reviewed in *Booklist*, August 1989.

Berger, Gilda, and Melvin Berger. **Drug Abuse A-Z.** Hillside, NJ: Enslow Publishers, 1990. 144p. $16.95. (A-Z Reference Series) LC 89-1512. ISBN 0-89490-193-1. (GR 6-12)

This is an easy-to-use guide to more than 1,000 drugs and drug-related terms. Entries list the scientific, trade, and slang names of the most frequently used drugs. Information is provided about prescription, over-the-counter, and street drugs as well as the special equipment and vocabulary involved in the drug culture and the effect of drugs on the brain and the body, both from regular doses and overdoses. Material is given on the history of major drug laws, and drugs are divided into eight categories. A list of government agencies and private organizations that provide information to teenagers is given.

Berger, Melvin. **Hazardous Substances: A Reference.** Hillside, NJ: Enslow Publishers, 1986. $12.95. LC 86-8806. ISBN 0-89490-116-8.

An alphabetical guide to more than 200 dangerous materials entered under the common name of the substance with cross references at entries for alternative names. Acronyms and chemical formulas are included as well as a directory of agencies to contact for further information. Also useful is the annotated list of federal laws and agencies that are responsible for the control of hazardous substances.

Bludworth, Edward G. **Three Hundred Most Abused Drugs: An Identification Handbook.** Sanford, FL: Trend House, 1985. 29p. illus. index. $3.50 pa. ISBN 0-9606732-1-0.

This publication is an updated edition of earlier, similar works that have been issued by other publishers. It contains color photographs of commonly abused drugs, many of them prescription tablets and capsules. Trade names, generic names, classification schedule numbers, ingredients, and amounts of each are indicated, with supplementary descriptions and a glossary of terms in separate sections. Publications such as this are very useful in helping laypersons, physicians, and law enforcement officers identify abused drugs, for instance those found in the possession of suspected drug users or pushers. Street drugs, though, are often disguised, and nearly impossible to identify except through chemical analysis, so this work will not identify all of them. A number of publications contain sections with similar photographs, but this compact booklet is as valuable as any.

Budavari, Susan, ed. **The Merck Index: An Encyclopedia of Chemicals, Drugs, and Biologicals.** 11th ed. Rahway, NJ: Merck, 1989. 1 vol. various pagings. illus. $35.00. LC 89-60001. ISBN 0-911910-28-X.

This index has been published for almost 100 years, written and edited by generations for Merck chemists. Intended for use by chemists, pharmacists, physicians, and others in allied professions, this compendium contains 10,000 entries of the most important chemicals, drugs, and biological substances with diagrams as well as molecular formula, drug code number, composition, molecular weight among others. Also included is foreign patent information. The back of the Index includes organic name reactions; a company register with name, city, and country; chemical abstracts names and registry numbers; a formula index; and a cross index of names.

Consumer Guide. **The New Prescription Drug Reference Guide.** Skokie, IL: Publications International, 1985. 438p. ISBN 0-8817-62466.

A remaking of the 1983 publication introducing the reader to drugs, allergic reactions, overdoses, and other drug-induced problems. Chapter titles include "Filling Your Prescription," "Administering Medication Correctly," "Coping with Side Effects," and "How Drugs Work." Having a prescription filled and administering medication correctly assures the best results from the drugs being taken. "Coping with Side Effects" of drugs and types of drugs includes obvious side effects, subtle side effects, drug use during pregnancy and breastfeeding, and the management of side effects. Effects are shown for cardiovascular drugs, drugs for the ears and eyes, gastrointestinal drugs, hormones, anti-infectives, anti-neoplastics, topical drugs, central nervous system drugs, respiratory drugs, and vitamins and minerals.

The major part of the volume consists of drug profiles: for each drug the brand name is given, with its manufacturer, the type of drug, its ingredients, the dosage forms, storage, uses, and treatment. Each side effect is given, both major and minor, and the way the medication interacts with other types of drugs is detailed. There is also a tablet/capsule identification guide, and a list of Canadian brand names. Finally, a lengthy series of warnings is presented including "Tell your doctor about unusual or allergic reactions you have had to any medications...." The glossary has approximately 300 terms.

Drug, Alcohol, and other Addictions: A Directory of Treatment Centers and Prevention Programs Nationwide. Phoenix, AZ: The Oryx Press, 1989. $45.00. LC 89-2867. ISBN 0-89774-416-0.

A comprehensive directory of listings of the names, addresses, and telephone numbers of nearly 18,000 facilities, centers, and programs. The entries have been chosen from local and state directories, from the yellow pages of telephone companies, from professional journals, and from the National

Institute of Drug Abuse's NDATUS, and intends to be comprehensive rather than evaluative. The names and titles of the appropriate contact persons and telephone hotlines are given. Features of the programs include addictions treated, treatment methods, number of clients in treatment, specialty groups served, ownership and sources of funding.

Reviewed in *Booklist*, August 1989.

Edelson, Edward. **ABCs of Prescription Drugs.** Garden City, NY: Doubleday, 1987. 275p. $12.95. LC 86-19845. ISBN 0-385-18558-8.

Part I includes "Prescription Drugs and You," part II "Diseases/Conditions" and "Drug Profiles." Appendixes cover foods and vitamins that may reduce or increase the effect of drugs, dangerous combinations of drugs and food, drugs absorbed more slowly with food, and drugs requiring vitamin supplements. Each entry gives the generic name, brand names, general precautions, common and less common side effects, drug interactions, effects of overdose, use during pregnancy and breast feeding, and use by older persons.

Hart, Stan. **Rehab: A Comprehensive Guide to the Best Drug-Alcohol Treatment Centers in the United States.** New York: Perennial Library, 1988. 528p. index. $22.95; $10.95 pa. LC 88-45033. ISBN 0-06-055133-X, 0-06-096296-8 pa.

A comprehensive listing of drug and alcoholism rehabilitation centers in the United States chosen, by the author's criteria, for a "full, tightly scheduled and balanced program ... love ... an attitude of caring and respect ... a therapeutic milieu ... simplicity ... and an overall sense of wellness...." The author personally visited the centers and interviewed staff before including them in this volume. The centers are mostly for adult inpatient treatment, although references are made to adolescent and outpatient programs.

For each entry, the name, address, and telephone number are given. The main entry includes the individual(s) interviewed, a brief description of the facility, its location, the length of treatment, cost, insurance accepted, residential accommodations, detox unit, age limitations, physical limitations, leaving the premises, gym and recreational program, whether there is a chapel on the premises, treatment, and the primary therapeutic staff. Also included are indications of programs for relapses, smoking regulations, decaffeinated or caffeinated coffee or sodas, the quality of the food, special units for women, and AA or such programs. Further information is provided on the family program, aftercare, whether there is a hospital on the premises, admitting hours, key personnel, telephone use, whether radios, stereos and cassettes are allowed, and visitation hours. Finally, the author includes comments and a rating of good, very good, or excellent. Six centers are listed for women only. A twenty-eight glossary and index (including only names of the centers by state) are found at the end of the book.

Information Please Almanac, Atlas and Yearbook. 1947- . Planned and supervised by Dan Golenpaul Associates. New York: Simon & Schuster, 1947. annual.

The 1989 edition of this yearbook had a special article, "Facts on Cocaine and Crack," from the National Institute on Drug Abuse. This article discussed

"What Is Cocaine?," "What Is Crack?," "How They Affect the Body," "The Danger of Taking These Drugs," "Effect on the Brain," "Risks Run by Pregnant Women," and "Treatment Programs." Further information appeared in the text under "Narcotics: Violations, Arrests for." Under "Liquor," statistics were given for age of purchase, economic factors, effects, law violations, moderation in use of, and taxes.

Keller, Mark, Mairi McCormick, and Vera Efron. **A Dictionary of Words about Alcohol.** 2d ed. New Brunswick, NJ: Rutgers Center of Alcohol Studies, 1982. 291p. bibliog. $19.50. LC 81-620046. ISBN 911290-12-5.

The authors of this unique work are authorities in the alcoholism field. They have defined all of the important words and terms relating to alcohol and the problems surrounding its use. Over 2,000 definitions are listed, including many slang expressions. The origin and preferred usage of terms are given, as are citations showing the work or term in context. In some instances, historical accounts are also included to show changes in meaning. A list of works cited has been appended. The material is presented on a scholarly level.

Lee, David. **Cocaine Handbook: An Essential Reference.** Berkeley, CA: And/Or Press, 1981. 201p. illus. bibliog. index. $19.95. LC 81-10865. ISBN 0-915904-68-3.

This is a revision of a 1976 publication called *Cocaine Consumer's Handbook*. The author, who died just before the new edition went to press, was concerned that the quality of cocaine on the illicit market had been deteriorating to the point where the consumer was fortunate to be able to obtain a product containing 50 percent cocaine. He assumed that adulterants used might be harmful (even though most of those mentioned are innocuous substances such as mannitol, lactose, or caffeine). In addition, of course, the buyer was being defrauded. The main purpose of the book is to show the reader how to avoid adulterated cocaine and provide techniques for refining the impure product.

The first chapter offers history and background information about the coca plant and cocaine. Chapter 2 discusses the various alkaloids of the coca plant and tells how they have been extracted using primitive methods. Chapter 3 is on the relationship of cocaine use to health, economics, and the law. An overview of the laws and penalties of the states of the U.S. is given in tabular format. Adulterants are discussed in chapter 5. Chapter 6, the main and longest section, describes tests used to determine cocaine quality. Some involve little more than casual inspection; others must be carried out in the laboratory. Photographic plates are provided showing test results. Chapter 7 is on purification. Appendixes include an essay on discontinuing cocaine abuse, a list of laboratories that analyze street drugs, a list of health centers that treat cocaine abusers, and a glossary. Included throughout in margins are quotations from various works on cocaine.

The book carries the usual disclaimer statement found in books of this kind, that the publishers and author do not condone or encourage the use of cocaine or any illegal substance, and it also warns that some of the documented analytical and purifying procedures involve extremely hazardous flammable substances. However, books of this kind do encourage the use of and experimentation with cocaine. Even though the work appears reasonably authentic and honest, it can have little other purpose than to assist users of cocaine—a basically dangerous and illegal substance.

NF

Lingeman, Richard R. **Drugs from A to Z: A Dictionary.** 2d ed., rev. and updated. New York: McGraw-Hill Book Co., 1974. 320p. bibliog. $9.95; $6.95 pa. LC 74-13363. ISBN 0-07-037913-0; 0-07-03791-1 pa.

Most of the terms included here are from the world of drug abuse, though some scientific and pharmacologic information about drugs, normal medical doses, history, and lore surrounding drugs of abuse, and quotations from the literature of the drug world are also included. The origins of the many slang terms listed are traced when possible. Eric Partridge's works on slang were consulted along with other works. The dictionary includes appendixes on nonsynthetic derivatives of opium, morphine, and cocaine; generic names of synthetic opiates; Schedule I drugs under the Controlled Substances Act of 1970; Schedule II drugs under the Controlled Substances Act of 1970, as revised in 1973; and Schedule III, IV, and V drugs under the Controlled Substances Act of 1970, as revised in 1973.

Narcotics and Drug Abuse A to Z. Queens Village, NY: Croner Publications, Inc., 1971- . Loose-leaf. 3v. Kept up-to-date with quarterly supplements. $54.95 per year per volume. LC 78-173860.

This is a loose-leaf directory, dictionary, and guide to information sources concerned with drug abuse. Each volume consists of several sections, including

(1) A dictionary section which explains about drugs as well as terms and slang expressions (including Spanish) used in the world of drug abuse.

(2) A narcotics and drug section which provides detailed profiles of the most abused substances (symptoms resulting from drug abuse are described and contrasted with similar symptoms resulting from various illnesses).

(3) A bibliography including audiovisual materials, articles, books, kits, records, and tapes related to drug abuse.

(4) Historical highlights of the drug abuse problem from 5000 B.C. to date, as well as a survey of the foreign drug scene, including existing legislation and penalties.

(5) A listing of programs and facilities, state penalties for possession of marijuana, and organizations concerned with drug abuse.

(6) A directory section listing treatment facilities, their services, admission requirements, and other pertinent data.

All sections are identical in each of the volumes except the directory of facilities and organizations, which varies according to the section of the country covered. The publication should be of particular value to judges, law enforcement agencies, guidance counselors, teachers, clergymen, and parents.

O'Brien, Robert, and Morris Chafetz, eds. **Encyclopedia of Alcoholism.** New York: Facts on File, 1983. 378p. $40.00. LC 81-12562. ISBN 0-87196-623-9.

This is the first volume in a series of encyclopedias prepared by Facts on File. This entry in the set will be readable for both layperson and professional.

Reviewed in *Booklist*, December 15, 1989.

O'Brien, Robert, and Sidney Cohen. **The Encyclopedia of Drug Abuse.** New York: Facts on File, 1985-1986. bibliog. index. 454p. $40.00. LC 82-5034. ISBN 0-87196-690-5.

This volume is written for both the layperson and the professional and is a compantion to the *Encyclopedia of Alcoholism* edited by O'Brien and Morris Chafetz. The encyclopedia begins with "The History of Drugs and Man" and a brief "Glance at the Future." A five-page "Drug Classification" covers antidepressants, antipsychotic tranquilizers, cannabis, combinations, hallucinogens, narcotic analgesic antagonists, narcotic antagonists, nonprescription analgesics, sedative/hypnotics, stimulants, and volatile inhalants. Entries are as short as three lines on the double-column page for "nystagmus" and as long as five columns for "withdrawal." Appendixes include "Street Language," "Slang Synonyms for Drugs," and fifty-five tables including "Drug Control Laws," "Drug Treatment Units," "Drug Users in Treatment," "Public Attitudes Toward Alcohol and Drugs," "Reported Patterns of Drug Use," "Trafficking in and Growth of Cocaine Abuse," and "Violations of Drug Laws." Sources of information include not only the United States but also Canada, international and foreign agencies and organizations, and major English-language journals, newspapers, and periodicals. The twenty-three-page bibliography is somewhat dated.

Physicians' Desk Reference for Nonprescription Drugs. 9th ed. Dradell, NJ: Medical Economics Co., 1990. $23.95. ISBN 0-87489-846-3.

This reference book is published annually to provide information on nonprescription drugs. The color-coded volume includes a manufacturers' index, product name index, product category index, active ingredients index, and sections on product identification, product information, diagnostics, devices and medical aids, educational material, and poison control centers. In "How to Use This Edition," the reader is told that drugs can be located by brand name of product if you know either the manufacturer's name or the generic name, by manufacturer's name if you know the product's brand or generic name, by a product with a chemical action if you know the chemical action, by a product with a particular active ingredient if you know the active ingredient, by a similar-acting product if you know the product classification, and by the generic name of a brand-name product if you know the product's brand name. Both the product's brand name and the product's generic name can lead the reader to the product's actions, warnings, drug interaction, precautions, symptoms and treatment of oral overdose, dosage and administration, and method of supply. Essential product information includes active ingredients, actions, warnings, interaction with other drugs, symptoms and treatment of oral overdosage, particular chemical actions, similar-acting products, and generic names of brand-name products. The section on product information entries contain the name of the company, the registered name, pronunciation, its form (vitamin and iron drops), active ingredients, its action and uses, its administration and dosage, and how supplied (tablet, tube, box), with warnings. Ingredients of the tablet may indicate the percentage of vitamins in each tablet.

The Manufacturers' Index contains the name of the company and its address, telephone numbers, and products available. Additional information for some entries includes where to call for medical emergencies, as well as sales information. A total of thirty-two poison control centers are listed in the Directory of Regional Poison Control Centers.

Schneider, Janet, and Bunny Porter-Shirley. **Peterson's Drug and Alcohol Programs and Policies at Four-Year Colleges.** Princeton, NJ: Peterson's Guides, 1989. 445p. tables. $19.95 pa. LC 89-8743. ISBN 0-87866-731-8.

This is the first college guide to give students, families, counselors, and college administrators information concerning drugs and alcohol education programs at four-year colleges in the United States. The guide, presenting about 900 colleges, is arranged in alphabetical order by the name of the college. For each entry, general information is given about the college including type of institution, founding date, degrees awarded, number of faculty and students, number of fraternities and sororities, and the percentage of men and women who are members. Also provided is the name of the person to contact with address and telephone number. Programs and policies from each college are given including education and training programs, types of support groups provided for both staff and students, services, and regulations and disciplinary action. Information is given on the methods used by the colleges to identify chemically dependent students and staff in the admissions process and on campus. A comparative table is given to show a comparison of the colleges and their regulations on alcohol in 19 categories. The appendix includes "Standards of the Network of Colleges and Universities Committed to the Elimination of Drugs and Alcohol Abuse."

Reviewed in *Booklist*, January 1, 1990.

Spencer, Michael. **Free Publications from U.S. Government Agencies: A Guide.** Englewood, CO: Libraries Unlimited, 1989. 123p. $14.50. LC 89-2744. ISBN 0-87287-622-5.

This is a guide to the publications of the world's largest publisher, the U.S. Government. The publications programs of more than fifty U.S. agencies are detailed with evaluative comments. Entries allow the reader access to thousands of publications. The volume is divided by subjects, one of which is alcohol and drug abuse. Ordering information is given for the materials, many of which are in pamphlet or vertical file format.

Reviewed in *Book Report*, January-February 1990.

Stafford, Peter. **Psychedelics Encyclopedia.** Rev. ed. Technical editor, Jeremy Bigwood. Los Angeles, CA: J. P. Tarcher, Inc.; distr. Houghton Mifflin Co., 1983. 420p. illus. bibliog. index. $12.95 pa. ISBN 0-87477-231-1.

Andrew Weil wrote the foreword to this book which reviews the literature on psychedelic substances, gives an account of their properties, traces the history of their use, and comments on social attitudes regarding them. The book makes a strong plea for allowing their use legally to explore human consciousness and to bring about mystical experiences. Psychedelics are presented in a favorable light. Various reviewers have called the first edition of the work "a gas to read ... hip ... witty ... a treasure chest of weird and wonderful information" and "a delightful Rabelaisian social history."

The views expressed are controversial and one-sided, as little is said about the dangers inherent in the use of such substances. Most of the literature references are to secondary sources that, like this book, may encourage experimentation with psychedelics. However, the book with its many illustrations is interesting and the historical viewpoint is good.

Statistical Abstract of the United States. U.S. Bureau of the Census. Washington, D.C.: Government Printing Office, 1879- . annual.

General up-to-date information including such headings as drugs (illegal): arrests, court cases, enforcement activities, cigarette smoking by sex and age, and current users of alcohol, marijuana, and cocaine. This compendium contains summary statistics on the political, social, and economic organization of the United States. It is a guide to further information in the references cited for each table.

Substance Abuse & Kids: A Directory of Education, Information, Prevention, and Early Intervention Programs. Phoenix, AZ: Oryx Press, 1989. 466p. $65.00. LC 89-8848. ISBN 0-89774-583-3.

A listing of 1,500 programs dealing with drugs, alcohol, and behavioral disorders in children eighteen years old and under. Each program listing includes education and information, seminars, conferences, referral, patient/client library, group and family counseling, coed or single-sex peer counseling, early intervention and identification, and client assessment. Educational materials available from the programs, fees, age groups and grade levels served, addictions or disorders treated, referral or admission requirements, program evaluation, method and effectiveness, and follow-up care are all covered in this volume.

Turner, Carlton E. **Cocaine: An Annotated Bibliography.** 2v. Jackson, MS: University of Mississippi by University Press of Mississippi, 1989. 1,364p. $125.00. LC 88-29584. ISBN 0-87805-382-4.

A comprehensive bibliography of 4,040 annotated citations dating from 1859 to 1986 on the literature on cocaine and coca, this was the result of ten year's research completed by the Research Institute of Pharmaceutical Sciences at the University of Mississippi. A brief history of cocaine is given. The first volume contains an alphabetical list of the citations by author. The second volume is the author and subject index with a reference to the annotation number. The citations from 1859 to 1949 are not included in the subject index. Since this is intended for the university audience, secondary schools would only purchase if demand was great enough to warrant the expense.

Reviewed in *Library Journal*, April 15, 1990.

World Almanac and Book of Facts. annual. New York: World-Telegram, 1968- .

This reference provides statistics on social, industrial, political, financial, religious, and educational matters, among others. Political organizations and societies are also included. It is a very useful and reliable collection of miscellaneous facts.

DATABASES

National Library of Medicine **MEDLARS** (Medical Literature Analysis and Retrieval System) and **HISTLINE** (History of Medicine Online). U.S. Department of Health and Human Services, U.S. National Library of Medicine.

The National Library of Medicine's History of Medicine Division is the source for the annual printed *Bibliography of the History of Medicine.* This database can be searched through MEDLARS and includes works on individuals, institutions, the medical profession, diseases, and drugs. HISTLINE holds over 80,000 references, is updated monthly, and expands at the rate of 5,500 records per year.

National Library of Medicine **MEDLINE** (MEDLARS ONLINE). U.S. Department of Health and Human Services, U.S. National Library of Medicine.

MEDLINE is a computer-readable database with over 6,000,000 references to worldwide biomedical journal literature from 1966 to the present. The database contains all citations published in *Index Medicus*, and nearly half of the records added since 1975 contain author abstracts. MEDLINE supplies references to articles from 3,200 journals on medicine (preclinical and clinical sciences), life sciences, and other health science topics published in the United States and seventy other countries. MEDLINE is indexed using NLM's Medical Subject Headings (MeSH). This database is updated monthly with more than 250,000 references added annually.

Records include the accession number, author, title, source journal, volume and issue numbers, page numbers, publication date, ISSN, language, and descriptors.

Additional information on databases may be found in appendix D.

3

Resources for Educators

The 1960s began a period of social rebellion in youth. The structure of behavior in schools was toppled as students fought for their right to dress without regard for dress codes. They fought for their right not to serve in the military forces, and when they did not win, they ignored their school's teaching of patriotism and moved to Canada. In their quest for the opportunity to control their destinies they left school, home, and families to join with other teenagers and college students in Haight-Ashbury and similar sections in other large cities where they melted into groups of other teenagers, all testing their independence, many becoming lost in the process. Some parents and educators began to acknowledge that not all alcohol and drug abuse was centered in these larger cities, but the problem remained in their schools and homes with the children who had not physically left. Parents blamed the schools, and school officials blamed parents, claiming that parents no longer supported the efforts of educators. In fact, many parents used legal means to halt any punishment for the misbehavior of their children.

At first the problem of rebellion surfaced on college campuses where students built cardboard shelters to live in while they protested a variety of evils on campus and in the greater world. Presidents of institutions of higher education were locked into or out of their offices. With the protests and the striving for independence, a market was perceived for rock concerts. Woodstock became synonymous with independence and unrestrained activities. Performers, noise, and drugs provided examples for an ever-younger audience until it was impossible not to acknowledge that drugs and alcohol use had moved to the high schools in all areas, rural and suburban as well as urban.

Kozicki described why teenagers use substances. He began, "Adolescence is a period of development during which the young person, no longer a child and more or less physiologically mature, must gradually loosen the ties...."[1] (The complete article may be found in appendix E.) Establishing themselves as independent human beings means trying to break away from home and parents. Interests expand socially, intellectually, and sexually; and these areas of interest become inextricably interwoven. The period of testing can include experimenting with a variety of substances that are harmful, impacting on the social, intellectual, and sexual activities of teenagers. Certainly the outcomes of these experiments have "life sentences." Teenage pregnancy has reached epidemic proportions, AIDS is an ominous threat, and the ever-lowering age when children try substances is frightening.

Alarming statistics are reported by the National Center for Educational Statistics (NCES) in a recent publication, *Youth Indicators, 1988.* "The percentage of students who reported having ever used illicit drugs increased from 1975 to 1980."[2] While students reporting the use of alcohol and marijuana declined after 1980, more than one-fourth of high school seniors had used marijuana in the past thirty days. The increase in the use of cocaine and crack can be documented. The fight to stop drugs through education seems to be less successful than was hoped. William J. Bennett, the nation's drug policy director, questions the effectiveness of drug education programs and has said, "children were more likely to respond to aggressive law enforcement and assured punishment."[3] His premise is that "ignorance is not the problem" and that children were being informed about the drug problem. To Mr. Bennett, the value of drug education was merely a "helpful auxiliary," and, given the choice between drug education and tough policy, he would choose tough policy. Statistics have not been gathered concerning the value of drug education programs.

A recent RAND Corporation study pointed out that "social-skills-based programs may prevent or decrease the use of cigarettes and marijuana among seventh and eighth graders but do not affect their alcohol consumption."[4] This report of Project ALERT, published in the March 16, 1990, issue of *Science* magazine, showed that the curriculum for twenty California and Oregon junior high schools in inner-city, suburban, and rural communities did not prevent non-smokers from trying cigarettes, but it did indicate 27 percent less use of cigarettes by the experimental group in comparison to the control group.

Another recent study of 17,000 high school students shows that some types of use by high school students continues to decrease. Since 1975, the National Institute on Drug Abuse (NIDA) has conducted an annual survey of high school seniors. The latest results show the number of seniors who had used drugs within the last year dropped to 35.4 percent. Students seemed to define "drugs" as illicit narcotics. Further use of alcoholic beverages in the last month declined from the peak of 72 percent in 1980. Tobacco use was reported at 29 percent this year, a percentage that has remained constant since 1981. "Crack" or rock cocaine remained at 1.4 percent and PCP increased from .03 percent to 1.4 percent. Decreases were shown in the use of other illicit drugs, marijuana, LSD, and cocaine. The most alarming statistics were that 58.7 percent of the students surveyed said that cocaine was fairly easy or very easy to obtain. One researcher commented that the decline in drug use was most likely the influence of anti-drug peer pressure, media influences, and drug education programs.

Providing guidance for secondary school students who need to know the dangers and outcomes of misbehavior is not a new approach for educators, and teaching about substance abuse is not new. Certainly, educators can and should address the problems related to substance abuse. They should respond rather than react to communities who argue that school programs are not and have not been effective. While educators can not be expected to solve the problem, they can work toward health awareness and can offer guidance concerning the legal ramifications of substance abuse.

Educators provide guidance for teenagers, and they do not expect the guidance counselors or health teachers or coaches to undertake all the responsibility. Each educator must be prepared to offer guidance in this very important area.

Guidance from adults takes many forms: advice, questions answered, awareness before and when problems arise, and, perhaps the most difficult yet the most important, providing role models. Finding materials to give information that is timely, relevant, and appropriate, stating facts without preaching, and, above all, presenting statistics that are accurate is not an easy task. A first step is for teachers to become aware of what is available. Library media specialists can help them learn what is available by providing the right information at the right time and at the right level both to help them understand their students and to help them provide accurate information to their students. It is the task of all educators to understand enough about the problem of substance abuse to be able to decide what is accurate.

Educators are given the responsibility for implementation of state and local mandates for substance abuse education. Superintendents and principals must help teachers integrate awareness programs into their already-complete curriculum areas. The primary focus of the materials cited below is the educator, but they should be of interest to parents also. *What Works: Schools without Drugs* is of primary interest. This book offers twelve recommendations. Those applying directly to the school include the following:

- Be knowledgeable about drugs and signs of drug use. When symptoms are observed, respond promptly.

- Determine the extent and character of drug use and establish a means of monitoring that use regularly.

- Establish clear and specific rules regarding drug use that include strong corrective actions.

- Enforce established policies against drug use fairly and consistently. Implement security measures to eliminate drugs on school premises and at school functions.

- Implement a comprehensive drug prevention curriculum from kindergarten through grade 12, teaching that drug use is wrong and harmful and supporting and strengthening resistance to drugs.

- Reach out to the community for support and assistance in making the school's antidrug policy and program work. Develop collaborative arrangements in which school personnel, parents, school boards, law enforcement officers, treatment organizations, and private groups can work together to provide necessary resources.

For a variety of reasons, many schools still need to develop substance abuse education programs or to develop the enforcement measures needed to cope with students who use alcohol, drugs, or other harmful substances. Teachers must learn how to recognize a drug sale when it is being conducted in the classroom, school cafeteria, or media center. Hopefully the materials suggested below will help with this.

NF
Anderson, Gary L. **Enabling in the School Setting.** Minneapolis, MN: The Johnson Institute, 1988. 40p. $2.75. ISBN 0-935908-43-9.

This pamphlet suggests that enabling systems in schools with alcohol and other drug problems closely parallel enabling systems in families. Questionnaires are given covering the enabling behaviors of administrators, teachers, pupil service workers, students, and parents as well as presentations of the specific forms of denial that characterize each group.

NF
Anderson, Gary L. **Solving Alcohol/Drug Problems in Your School.** Minneapolis, MN: The Johnson Institute, 1988. 32p. $2.50. ISBN 0-935908-44-7.

This pamphlet describes the steps some schools have taken to deal with alcohol and drug use by students. Explanations are given for why these schools have not met expectations with suggestions for programs that are more effective. The author implies that these more useful programs cover all aspects of the problem because they involve parents, schools, and the community.

NF
Anderson, Gary L. **When Chemicals Come to School: The Student Assistant Program Model: A Comprehensive Guide to Student Assistance Programming for Educators Concerned About Alcohol and Other Drug Abuse.** Rev. ed. Greenfield, WI: Community Recovery Press, 1988. 478p. $29.95. LC 87-148398. ISBN 0-9618-023-1-6.

A step-by-step manual describing how to design, implement, and maintain student-assisted substance abuse programs. Resources and relevant statistics are shown, and educators are reminded that effective alcohol and other drug programming involves prevention, intervention, treatment, and support components. Further, such a program must be a joint school and community effort.

FLM/VHS
Choices and Consequences: Intervention with Youth in Trouble with Alcohol/Drugs. Minneapolis, MN: The Johnson Institute, 1989. 33 min. film, $525.00; video, $495.00.

A special intervention approach showing parents, teachers, and others methods to help teenagers at any level of alcohol or other drug use stop substance abuse. It also teaches students to stop enabling their friends and help them to stop drug abuse. This film is a companion to the book by Schaefer, *Choices & Consequences*, cited on page 88.

NF
Fleming, Martin. **Conducting Support Groups for Students Affected by Chemical Dependence: A Guide for Educators and Other Professionals.** Minneapolis, MN: The Johnson Institute, 1990. 160p. $12.95. ISBN 0-935908-51-X.

The author of this book explains in clear, nontechnical language the steps to follow to start a student support group. A brief overview discusses how student support groups work, what they offer to each student, how to form a group, and how to expand groups into a program. A detailed format is given to follow for each kind of group. Session-by-session goals are outlined, and the activities to reach the goals are described. A list of useful resources is given at the end of the book.

NF
Narcotics and Drug Abuse A to Z. Queens Village, NY: Croner Publications, Inc., 1971- . Loose-leaf. 3v. Kept up-to-date with quarterly supplements. $54.95 per year per volume. LC 78-173860.

See chapter 2: Reference Works for complete annotation.

VHS
Physiological Effects of Cocaine. New York: Hazleton Educational Materials, 1984. 20 min. video. $195.00.

The film discusses cocaine's effects upon the human body. The history and physical properties of cocaine are examined, and the physiological information can help chemical dependency counselors treat addicts.

NF
Prevention Research Findings, 1988: Proceedings of the First National Conference on Prevention Research Findings; Implications for Alcohol and Other Drug Abuse Program Planning. Rockville, MD: U.S. Department of Health, Public Health Service, [1990]. OSAP Prevention Monograph No. 3. 267p. free. LC 89-081212.

Contents include "State and Federal Roles in Prevention," "Prevention Research Perspectives," "School-Based Prevention Programs," "Community-Based Prevention Programs," "Health Promotion and Wellness," and "Public Policy Prevention Programs." The papers include extensive bibliographies, tables, and charts.

NF
Sasatelli, Jean. **Breaking Away: Saying Good-bye to Alcohol/Drugs.** Minneapolis, MN: The Johnson Institute, 1989. 24p. $2.95. ISBN 0-935908-47-1.

This brief pamphlet is helpful to teachers who wish to show students how their relationship to chemicals has hurt their relationships with family and friends.

NF

Schaefer, Dick. **Choices & Consequences: What to Do When a Teenager Uses Alcohol/Drugs: A Step-by-Step System That *Really* Works.** Minneapolis, MN: The Johnson Institute, 1988. 156p. $9.95. LC 87-22717. ISBN 0-935908-42-0.

Provides teachers, parents, and other professionals with methods to stop a teenager's chemical use at any stage from early experimentation to harmful dependence. Going beyond "just say no" this system is designed to help teenagers want and choose to get off and stay off alcohol and other drugs. A companion to the film, *Choices and Consequences*, cited earlier.

NF

Schlaadt, Richard B., and Peter T. Shannon. **Drugs of Choice: Current Perspectives on Drug Use.** 2d ed. Englewood Cliffs, NJ: Prentice-Hall, Inc., 1986. 320p. illus. charts. diagrams. bibliog. index. $19.95. LC 85-17001. ISBN 0-13-220740-0.

See chapter 1: General Collection for complete annotation.

NF

Schwebel, Robert. **Saying No Is Not Enough: Raising Children Who Make Wise Decisions about Drugs and Alcohol.** New York: Newmarket Press, 1989. 256p. $17.95. LC 89-33775. ISBN 1-55704-041-9.

Helping children to become empowered by acquiring positive life skills will prepare them to make wise decisions concerning substance abuse. The author of this book is a drug counselor and psychologist who believes that something less simple than "just say no" is required to help children "say no." Presenting the case that drugs are not necessarily "everywhere" and that "drug use is not inevitable," parents are encouraged to open discussion with their children, establishing a no-drugs standard in the home, and keeping communication open.

Reviewed in *Library Journal*, October 15, 1990.

NF

What Works: Schools without Drugs. Washington, D.C.: U.S. Department of Education, 1986. 78p. free.

From the introduction by then-Secretary of Education William J. Bennett, this small booklet covers "What Can We Do" as parents, schools, students, and communities. Special sections cover teaching about prevention and how the law can help. Eight pages are used to describe specific drugs and their effects by type, what they may be renamed, what they look like, and how they are used. A copy may be obtained by writing the Consumer Information Center, Pueblo, CO 81003.

NOTES

[1] Zigmond A. Kozicki. "Why Do Adolescents Use Substances (Drugs/ Alcohol)," *Journal of Alcohol and Drug Education* 32 (Fall 1986): 1.

[2] *Youth Indicators 1988: Trends in the Well-Being of American Youth.* (Washington, D.C.: U.S. Department of Education, 1988.), 99.

[3] Richard L. Berke. "Bennett Doubts Value of Drug Education," *New York Times* 3 February 1990, national edition.

[4] *Drug Prevention Curriculum: A Guide to Selection and Implementation.* (Washington, D.C.: Office of Educational Research and Improvement, U.S. Department of Education, 1988.), 41-42.

4

Resources for Parents

From the "terrible twos" until age ten, parents usually feel in control of their children. As these same parents watch their sons and daughters enter middle school and junior high, the influence peers begin to assert may not be recognized by adult or adolescent. Yet it is there, and the child begins to claim a share of independence.

Kozicki states that "Adolescence is a period of development during which the young person, no longer a child and more or less physiologically mature, must gradually loosen the ties which have bound him/her to the home and to his/her parents."[1] The methods they use to loosen those ties begin at home for that is where the binding is perceived to be, and the persons who hold those ties are parents.

Parents have the most direct influence on their children. As the television commercial shows, a child can most easily learn how to abuse substances by watching a parent who drinks or smokes too much or who is a drug user. Research has confirmed that "the first influence on alcohol, marijuana, and substance usage was the parents, and the second strongest influence was peers,"[2] and "parental use of drugs has an impact on their adolescents. Greater illicit drug use by parents correlated with their adolescents' use of illegal drugs."[3]

For those parents who are models of abstinence, the concern is always there that a child will become a substance abuser.

No information is available in any format that can guarantee parents will be able to identify substance abuse by their children. However, the materials here will help parents become knowledgeable about types of abuse, the vocabulary and signs of substance abuse, and sources of help if they think their children may have a problem.

MEDIA

NF

Ackerman, Robert J. **Children of Alcoholics: A Guide for Parents, Educators, and Therapists.** 2d ed. New York: Simon & Schuster, 1987. 224p. filmography. bibliog. index. (A Learning Publication/Fireside Book) $7.95 pa. LC 87-8514. ISBN 0-671-64527-7. (GR 9-adult)

The cover of this book adds "How to Help and Find Help for Children Trapped in Alcoholic Families" as a further description of the contents. The book is divided into three parts, "The Child of an Alcoholic: What It's Like," "Suggestions for Educators," and "Suggestions for Therapists and Parents." Facts lead into further narrative: "If a woman is married to a male alcoholic and there are children under the age of eighteen in the family, nine out of ten women will stay with the alcoholic. However, if the situation is reversed, and she is the alcoholic, only one out of ten males will stay." Included are questions for the family to help them go beyond the denial stage.

The section for administrators suggests that "a deservable program that meets the needs of students with alcoholic parents will be mutually supported by school administrators and their staffs." It includes suggestions for in-service training, development of resources, and setting a school's policy on the program as formal or informal. The next chapter covers what can be done "Outside of the Classroom."

Parents are encouraged not to feel alone. A list of ten points covers what the parent can do, beginning with "Be flexible regarding the demands that you make on yourself and your children remembering that problematic situations call for adaptable measures," and closing with "Get help! NOW!" The appendixes include a bibliography of books, sources of pamphlets and booklets, suggested films and videocassettes, and resource agencies.

VHS

Adult Children of Alcoholics. Van Nuys, CA: AIMS Media, 1988. 30 min. $325.00.

See chapter 1: General Collection for complete annotation.

NF

Andre, Pierre, M.D. **Drug Addiction: Learn about It Before Your Kids Do.** Pompano Beach, FL: Health Communications, 1987. 117p. appendixes. bibliog. $7.95 pa. LC 87-21205. ISBN 0-932194-58-3.

The author, a medical doctor, answers questions about cocaine addiction and presents a guide for parents for assessing cocaine dependence in their children. The effects of drug addiction on family members are given as well as lists of treatment centers.

Reviewed in *Booklist*, December 15, 1987 and *Library Journal*, January 1988.

NF

Bartimole, Carmella, and John Bartimole. **Teenage Alcoholism and Substance Abuse: Causes, Cures, and Consequences.** Hollywood, FL: Frederick Fell Publishers, 1987. 125p. $6.95 pa. LC-86-4229. ISBN 0-936320-18-4.

The title page describes the volume as "a handbook for parents of teenagers that explores the reasons that teens become involved with drugs and alcohol and how to prevent it." Chapter titles are "Teenage Alcoholism and

Substance Abuse: An Overview," "The Language of Drugs," "The Short- and Long-Term Effects of Drugs," "Alcohol and Its Effects," "The Warning Signs of Substance Abuse," "Why Kids Do Drugs and Alcohol," "If You Suspect Your Child Is Abusing Drugs," "What Parents Can Do to Help Prevent Alcohol and Substance Abuse," "What Schools Must Do to Help," and "Where Do We Go from Here?" Tables list depressants, hallucinogens, inhalants, cannabis, stimulants, and narcotics, describing for each the trade or street name, possible signs of abuse, and a rating for both physical and psychological dependence. The vocabulary makes the book quick reading.

NF
Barun, Ken, and Philip Bashe. **How to Keep the Children You Love Off Drugs: A Prevention and Intervention Guide for Parents of Preschoolers, School-agers, Preteens, and Teens.** New York: Atlantic Monthly Press, 1988. 266p. $12.95. LC 88-3376. ISBN 0-87224-1803.

Barun, Ken, and Philip Bashe. **When Saying No Isn't Enough: How to Keep the Children You Love Off Drugs.** New York: New American Library, 1989. 351p. appendixes. bibliog. $4.95 pa. ISBN 0-45116-1386.

Popularly written books published in hardbound under the first title and paperback under the second, these titles are a combination of statistics, information, definitions, and case studies to help parents understand the problem of drug abuse. The first page of text quotes the National Institute of Drug Abuse and the National Council on Alcoholism: "the average age of first drug use is now thirteen, and of first alcohol use, twelve."

Individuals who have struggled with their own drug problems sometimes evolve into knowledgeable experts on the subject. One of the authors, Ken Barun, is no exception. He has been a drug abuser. Touted now as the nation's leading fighter against drug abuse, he tells parents how to guide their children safely through their "drug susceptible" years, ages eight to twenty. Much of the books are in the familiar but effective mode: "I acquired my substance-abuse education the hard way, nearly dying in the process." The books contain a great deal of information and can be read quickly and easily, including why children go on drugs, facts about the drugs they use, parents' all-too-common mistakes, how to make your child want to say no to drugs, tell-tale signs of drug use, how to respond, and names and addresses of drug abuse programs nationwide. Parents will be interested in the contents.

NF
Daley, Dennis C., and Judy Miller. **A Parent's Guide to Alcoholism & Drug Abuse: Practical Advice for Recovery & Relapse Prevention.** Newport, RI: Edgehill Publications, 1989. $6.95 pa. LC 89-83896. ISBN 0-926028-01-4.

This book focuses on parents who have chemically dependent sons or daughters. The authors feel that this group is very often overlooked. It has been the experience of Daley and Miller that parents experience turmoil and distress when a son or daughter is chemically dependent. *A Parent's Guide to Alcoholism and Drug Abuse* was written as a resource guide for parents who are involved with recovery programs. The chapters include "Understanding Chemical Dependency," "Your Chemically Dependent Child—How Bad Is the Problem?," "Your Family—What has Chemical Dependency Done to It?,"

"Effects of Chemical Dependency on Parents—Identifying How You Have Been Affected," "Your Chemically Dependent Child—Recovery and Relapse Prevention," and "Recovery and Relapse Prevention for Parents."

NF

Daley, Dennis C. **Surviving Addiction: A Guide for Alcoholics, Drug Addicts, and Their Families.** New York: Gardner Press, Inc., 1988. 251p. index. $19.95. LC 87-21106. ISBN 0-89876-146-8.

Through case studies, basic information is presented on addiction, for example, how users become addicted, effects, rehabilitation, relapse, and the role of family. The volume is divided into four parts: "Introduction to Addiction," "The Alcoholic and Drug Addict," "The Family," and "Conclusions." Within these parts topics covered include "Alcohol and Drug Addiction: Diseases That Affect Everyone," "How People Become Addicted and Stay That Way," "The Effects of Addiction on the Alcoholic or Drug-Addicted Person," "Getting Well: The Recovery Journey," "Relapse Prevention: Reserving a Seat on the Recovery Wagon," "Where to Get Help: Programs for Alcoholics and Drug Addicts," "Getting the Alcoholic or Drug Addict to Accept Help," "What Addiction Really Does to the Family," "Living on a Roller Coaster: Being Married to an Alcoholic or Drug Addict," "Innocent Victims: The Children," "Recovery of the Family," "Family Relapse Prevention," and "Where the Family Can Get Help." The appendix includes a bibliography with 114 entries coded by the intended audience, helping understand addiction and recovery, effects on family, effects on young children, and effects on adult children as well as the twelve steps of Alcoholics Anonymous, and a list of publishers of information on addiction and recovery.

NF

Ellis, Barbara Gray. **Drug Abuse from the Family Perspective.** Rockville, MD: National Institute on Drug Abuse, Office of Program Development and Analysis, 1980. DHHS Publication No. (ADM) 80-910.

This is a collection of commissioned papers on topics such as "Some Overlooked Aspects of the Family and Drug Abuse," "Hispanic Family Factors and Drug Abuse," "Family Therapy and the Chicano Drug Abuser," "Treating Adolescent Drug Abuse as a Symptom of Dysfunction in the Family," and "Family Counseling for Low-Income Drug Abusers." The final paper is a "Report of a Workshop on Reinforcing the Family System as the Major Resource in the Primary Prevention of Drug Abuse."

NF

Forrest, Gary G. **How to Cope with a Teenage Drinker: New Alternatives and Hope for Parents and Families.** New York: Atheneum, 1983. 174p. $10.50. LC 82-73023. ISBN 0-689-11346-3.

See chapter 1: General Collection for complete annotation.

VHS

High on Life Not on Drugs: A Guide for Teens. Grand Rapids, MI: The Training Resource Inc., 1987. Distributed by Spin, Inc., P.O. Box 2589, Littleton, CO 80161. 35 min.

The jacket on this video states that "Every student ... Every law enforcement officer ... Every teacher ... Every parent should see this program!" The video is introduced by the former head of the federal Drug Enforcement Administration who was also a former FBI official. The remainder of the video features a police officer from Kingsport, Tennessee, Sergeant Bud Hulsey, who presents with a very rapid, crisp discourse before a live audience. The premise of the video is that the basic reason teenagers use drugs is boredom. The video would be more successful for a parents' group than for students.

NF
Johnson, Vernon. **Everything You Need to Know about Chemical Dependence.** Minneapolis, MN: The Johnson Institute, 1990. 496p. $19.95. LC 90-4164. ISBN 0-935908-53-6.

This book is designed for families to provide them with information before, during, and after trouble begins. Questions concerning recognizing chemical dependence, avoiding dependence, helping the family solve problems related to substance abuse, and how to prevent children from using drugs are answered. Contents include "Chemical Dependence in Individuals," "Effects of Chemical Dependence at Home and at Work," "Children of Alcoholics," "Intervention: How to Help Someone Who Doesn't Want Help," and "How Parents Can Prevent Chemical Dependence in Their Children." National organizations to contact are also listed.

NF
Ketcham, Katherine, and Ginny Lyford Gustafson. **Living on the Edge: A Guide to Intervention for Families with Drug and Alcohol Problems.** New York: Bantam, 1989. 256p. bibliog. $8.95 pa. LC 88-7723. ISBN 0-553-34606-7. (GR 9-12)

See chapter 1: General Collection for complete annotation.

NF
Levy, Stephen J. **Managing the "Drugs" in Your Life: A Personal and Family Guide to the Responsible Use of Drugs, Alcohol, Medicine.** New York: McGraw-Hill, 1983. 330p. bibliog. index. $16.95. LC 82-24951. ISBN 0-07-037411-2.

See chapter 1: General Collection for complete annotation.

NF
Narcotics and Drug Abuse A to Z. Queens Village, NY: Croner Publications, Inc., 1971- . Loose-leaf. 3v. Kept up to date with quarterly supplements. $54.95 per year per volume. LC 78-173860.

See chapter 2: Reference Works for complete annotation.

VHS
A Nightmare on Drug Street. Produced by Twin Tower Enterprises, Search Foundation, and Universal/MCA. Twin Tower, 1988. video. $19.95.

This video was produced for the home market and, as such, cannot be used in public or school libraries without obtaining special permission. This is not the forum to discuss violating copyright, but special permission might be granted if requested. The scenario is of one near-teenager and two teenagers who are "dead." Representing both sexes and three ethnic backgrounds, they relate their drug- and alcohol-abusing lives. Parental denial, peer pressure, and their finding out too late that substance abuse is not a way to solve problems are presented. Since all three come from an affluent neighborhood, the video may not be as useful in the inner city. However, their deaths are from causes common to substance abuse: one is killed driving drunk, another by an overdose of pills and cocaine, and the third by a heart attack after using crack.

Reviewed in *School Library Journal*, December 1989.

NF

Polson, Beth, and Newton Miller. **Not My Kid: A Parent's Guide to Kids and Drugs.** New York: Avon Books, 1985. 224p. $4.50 pa. ISBN 0-380-69997.

Gripping portrayal of the widespread problem of drug abuse. The problem is so insidious that ordinary household products are being abused. For example, kids paint cigarettes with toothpaste and smoke dried banana peels to get high. Polson identifies patterns and signals parents should be alerted to—both physical and behavioral clues. Polson takes us through various aspects of the family drug problem: parent denial, kid denial, parent and societal enablers, strategy for action, and how to get outside help and treatment. The authors have included a helpful slang glossary, an appendix of further readings, and an index.

NF

Rosenbloom, Jonathan, ed. **Helping Your Child Say No to Alcohol.** Washington, D.C.: U.S. Department of Health and Human Services, 1987. DHHS Publication No. (ADM) 87-1500.

Distributed by the National Clearinghouse for Alcohol Information, this pamphlet was prepared by the Children's Television Workshop. Topics include "I drink, so how can I tell my child not to?" and "Ten steps to help your preteen say no." Seven reasons are presented for why kids drink, and the effects of alcohol on the brain and body are given. Keeping communication lines open to children and helping them build self-confidence are suggested as means to help children deal with peer pressure. Discussion presents methods for what to do if you think your child is drinking and how to maintain family ties. The final suggestion is to discuss ads with children asking them if they understand that ads are to sell products and to have them discuss the ads for alcoholic beverages. Resource groups available for parents are given with addresses and telephone numbers for the headquarters office.

NF

Schlaadt, Richard B., and Peter T. Shannon. **Drugs of Choice: Current Perspectives on Drug Use.** 2d ed. Englewood Cliffs, NJ: Prentice-Hall, Inc., 1986. 320p. illus. charts. diagrams. bibliog. index. $19.95. LC 85-17001. ISBN 0-13-220740-0.

See chapter 1: General Collection for complete annotation.

NF

Schwebel, Robert. **Saying No Is Not Enough: Raising Children Who Make Wise Decisions about Drugs and Alcohol.** New York: Newmarket Press, 1989. 256p. $17.95. LC 89-33775. ISBN 1-55704-041-9.

See chapter 3: Resources for Educators for complete annotation.

NF
Wilmes, David J. **Parenting for Prevention: How to Raise a Child to Say No to Alcohol/Drugs for Parents, Teachers, and Other Concerned Adults.** Minneapolis, MN: The Johnson Institute, 1988. 200p. $9.95. LC 88-8245. ISBN 0-935908-46-3.

This book shows how parents can take the lead in preventing their children from becoming involved with alcohol and other drugs. New insights and practical skills for parenting problems are given. Suggestions are given for helping children develop positive attitudes, feelings, and behaviors; handle stress, become confident, and gain self-reliance; communicate effectively with others; learn to live happily and productively as individuals and group members; set goals and reach them; manage time well; build a supportive network of family and friends; and take responsibility for their feelings, thoughts, and actions.

NF
Youcha, Geraldine, and Judith S. Seixas. **Drugs, Alcohol and Your Children: How to Keep Your Family Substance-Free.** New York: Crown, 1989. 224p. index. $15.95. LC 88-20218. ISBN 0517-57102-1. (adult)

Parents may find themselves with children with substance abuse problems or with a child who is in prison for drug dealing. This three-part book attempts to explain to parents what they should look for and what they should do. Chapters include "What's Really Happening," "Why My Kid?," "Warning Signs," "Talking and Listening—the Two-Way Street," "Parent Power," "The Law: Knowing It and Using It," "Family Fallout," "Grown-Up Children/Puzzled Parents," and "Finding the Right Help." The final part includes a drug dictionary with long definitions to fifty-three terms. A total of thirty-seven books are listed in the suggested readings. Brief references are given to where to get information and help, mainly the addresses to agencies discussed in the text. Free information sources include the name of the helpline or agency, the address, and a brief statement of what is available. Finally, the section on where to call for catalogs on drug and alcohol abuse lists seven sources by name and telephone number.

ORGANIZATIONS FOR PARENTS

The following organizations for parents are listed here as a convenience. Their complete addresses can be found in chapter 5, Free and Inexpensive Material.

Adult Children of Alcoholics

Al-Anon Family Group Headquarters

Cocanon Family Groups

Families in Action

Just Say No Foundation

Nar-Anon Family Group Headquarters

National Federation of Parents For Drug-Free Youth
National Hispanic Families Against Drug Abuse
Pride
Veteran's Administration

NOTES

[1] Zigmond A. Kozicki, "Why Do Adolescents Use Substances (Drugs/Alcohol)," *Journal of Alcohol and Drug Education* 32 (Fall 1986): 1.

[2] Mark A. Halebsky, "Adolescent Alcohol and Substance Abuse: Parent and Peer Effects." *Adolescence.* 22 (Winter 1987): 963.

[3] Ibid., 965.

5

Free and Inexpensive Materials

Sources of free and inexpensive materials on substance abuse may be requested from the following agencies:

AGENCIES

AAA Foundation for Traffic Safety
1730 M Street NW
Washington, D.C. 20036

Alberta Alcoholism and Drug Abuse Commission
Box 2900
Main Post Office
Edmonton, Alberta T5J2G5
Canada

Action on Smoking and Health
2013 H Street NW
Washington, D.C. 20006

Adult Children of Alcoholics
Suite 200
2522 West Sepulveda Boulevard
Torrance, CA 90505

Alcoholics Anonymous
Box 459
Grand Central Station
New York, NY 10163

Al-Anon/Alateen
Family Group Headquarters, Inc.
7th Floor
1372 Broadway
New York, NY 10018-0862

Alcohol and Drug Problems Association
4144 North Capitol Street NW
Suite 181
Washington, D.C. 20001

American Cancer Society
777 Third Avenue
New York, NY 10017

American Council for Drug Education
204 Monroe Street
Suite 110
Rockville, MD 20850

American Heart Association
7320 Greenville Avenue
Dallas, TX 75231

American Lung Association
1740 Broadway
New York, NY 20019

Arrive Alive America
P.O. Box 1185
Decatur, GA 30031-1185

Boy Scouts of America
Drug Abuse Task Force S200
1325 Walnut Hill Lane
Irving, TX 75038-3096

The Chemical People/WQED
4802 Fifth Avenue
Pittsburgh, PA 15213

Chemical Specialties Manufacturers Association, Inc.
1001 Connecticut Avenue, NW
Washington, D.C. 20036

Cocaine Anonymous Central Office
6125 Washington Boulevard
Suite 202
Culver City, CA 92030

Cocanon Family Groups
P.O. Box 64742-66
Los Angeles, CA 90064

COSSMHO (Coalition of Hispanic Health and Human Services Organizations)
1030 15th St., NW
Suite 1053
Washington, D.C. 20005

Drug Enforcement Administration
U.S. Dept. of Justice
1405 I Street NW
Washington, D.C. 20537

Families Anonymous, Inc.
P.O. Box 528
Van Nuys, CA 91408

Families in Action
Suite 201
2296 Henderson Mill Road
Atlanta, GA 30345

Girl Scouts of the U.S.A.
830 Third Avenue
New York, NY 10022

Governor's Traffic Safety Council
Transportation & Safety Bldg.
Harrisburg, PA 17120

Group Against Smoking Pollution
Box 682
College Park, MD 20740

Institute on Black Chemical Abuse
2614 Nicollet Ave.
Minneapolis, MN 55408

Insurance Institute for Highway Safety
1005 N. Glebe Road
Arlington, VA 22201

The Just Say No Foundation
Suite 210
1777 North California Boulevard
Walnut Creek, CA 94596

Mothers Against Drunk Driving
MADD National Office
669 Airport Freeway, Suite 310
Hurst, TX 76053

Nar-Anon Family Group Headquarters
World Service Office
P.O. Box 2562
Palos Verdes Peninsula, CA 92704

National Association for Children of Alcoholics
31706 Coast Highway, Suite 201
South Laguna, CA 92677

National Association of Broadcasters
1771 N Street NW
Washington, D.C. 20036

The National Association of State Alcohol and Drug Abuse Directors
Suite 530
444 North Capitol Street, NW
Washington, D.C. 20001

National Black Organizations Against Alcohol and Drug Use
22 Chapel Street
Brooklyn, NY 11201

National Clearinghouse for Alcohol and Drug Information
P.O. Box 2345
Rockville, MD 20852

National Clearinghouse for Drug Abuse Information
Box 416
Kinsington, MD 20795

National Clearinghouse for the Prevention of Drug and Alcohol Abuse
c/o The Quest
National Center
6655 Sharon Woods Blvd.
Chicago, IL 60611

National Commission Against Drunk Driving
1140 Connecticut Avenue, NW
Suite 804
Washington, D.C. 20036

National Council on Alcoholism
1511 K Street NW
Suite 320
Washington, D.C. 20005

National Crime Prevention Council
Room 540
733 15th Street, NW
Washington, D.C. 20005

National Federation of Parents for Drug-Free Youth
8730 Georgia Ave.
Suite 200
Silver Spring, MD 20910

National Highway Traffic Safety Administration
400 Seventh Street, SW
Washington, D.C. 20590

National Highway Traffic Safety Administration
Office of Alcohol and State Programs—NTS 21
400 Seventh Street, SW
Washington, D.C. 20590
Attn: Legislative Resource Center (to get copy of annual digest of State Alcohol-Safety Legislation)

National Hispanic Families Against Drug Abuse
1511 K Street NW
Washington, D.C. 20005

National Institute on Alcohol Abuse and Alcoholism
5600 Fishers Lane
Rockville, MD 20857

National Institute on Drug Abuse
P.O. Box 416
Kensington, MD 20795

National Organization for Victim Assistance
717 D Street NW
Washington, D.C. 20004

National Parents' Resource Institute for Drug Education (PRIDE)
Robert W. Woodruff (Building) Volunteer Service Center
100 Edgewood Ave., N.E.
Suite 1002
Atlanta, GA 30303

National Prevention Network
444 North Capitol St., NW
Suite 530
Washington, D.C. 20001

National PTA Drug Alcohol Abuse Prevention Project
700 North Rush Street
Chicago, IL 60611

National Safety Council
1705 DeSales Street, NW
Suite 300
Washington, D.C. 20036

National Self-Help Clearinghouse
33 West 42nd Street
Room 1222-A
New York, NY 10036

National Transportation Safety Board
SP-10
800 Independence Avenue, SW
Washington, D.C. 20594

Office of Smoking and Health
U.S. Department of Health and Human Services
110 Park Building
5600 Fishers Lane
Rockville, MD 20857

Office of Substance Abuse Prevention
5600 Fishers Lane
Parklawn Building, Room 13A54
Rockville, MD 20857

Students Against Driving Drunk
Box 800
Marlboro, MA 01752

Texans' War on Drugs
11044 Research Blvd., Bldg. D
Austin, TX 78759-5239

U.S. Department of Education Alcohol and Drug Abuse Education Program
400 Maryland Avenue, SW
Washington, D.C. 20202

Veterans Administration Alcohol and Drug Dependent Service
810 Vermont Ave., NW
Washington, D.C. 20420

Wisconsin Clearinghouse for Alcohol and Other Drug Information
1954 E. Washington Avenue
Madison, WI 53704

1-800-COCAINE
Fair Oaks Hospital
19 Prospect Street
Summit, NJ 07901

PAMPHLET SOURCES

The following are sources of pamphlets on substance abuse. Cost of these is included in the annotation rather than in the citation. Other pamphlets and materials may be gathered from the list in appendix F, Sources of Information, or in the Introduction, where government documents are presented.

Channing L. Bete Co., Inc.
200 State Road
South Deerfield, MA 01373
(413-665-7611 or 800-628-7733)

Most scriptographic booklets are 5½" x 8" with sixteen pages. Booklets can be used for curriculum components, for displays, for materials to distribute, or for impetus for class discussions. The company will personalize the booklets with special messages, logos, or other material on the front or back. The cost varies according to quantity. Most start at $.72 to $1.05 each. Foreign language editions are also available.

Greenhaven Press, Inc.
P.O. Box 289009
San Diego, CA 92128-9009
(619-485-7424 or 800-231-5163)

Opposing Viewpoints pamphlets are reprints of individual chapters from the Opposing Viewpoints Book Series including abuse topics. Cost of each is $2.45 or they may be purchased as a set for $78.40.

Life Skills Education
226 Libbey Parkway
Weymouth, MA 02189
(617-337-7828)

Up-to-date and accurate pamphlets in a 5½" x 8½", sixteen-page format. Pamphlets may be personalized with name or logo. Prices start at $1.35 each for pamphlets and $.35 each for flyers. Orders are accepted for a minimum of fifty flyers.

Public Affairs Pamphlets
381 Park Avenue South
New York, New York 10016

Timely, reliable, concise information in a handy format. An example is "Hill, Margaret. Drugs-Use, Misuse, Abuse: Guidance for Families. #515A, 1974, 1985, 24 pp. ISBN 0-88291-012.4 and Saltman, Jules. Teenagers and Alcohol: Patterns and Dangers." This costs $1.00 each and discounts are given for quantity.

Rutgers Center of Alcohol Studies
P.O. Box 969
Piscataway, NJ 08855

Pamphlets are designed to present technical information about alcohol use and abuse. Examples include: Brick, John. "Drugs and the Brain: An

Introduction to Neuropharmacology." 13pp. #QPP-341, and Russell, Robert D. "What Shall We Teach the Young About Drinking?" 19pp. #QPP-344. Pamphlets are priced at $2.50 each.

William Gladden Foundation
79 Carley Avenue
Huntington, NY 11743
(516-673-4584)

This is a non-profit organization that uses the proceeds from sales to advance research on juvenile delinquency and other children's issues. Examples include two pamphlets by Wain K. Brown, *When Children Use Drugs* and *Underage Drinking*. Both pamphlets are twenty pages in length and are priced at $2.95 each. Quantity discounts are also available.

Winters Communications, Inc.
1007 Samy Drive
Tampa, FL 33613
(813-962-0289)

Pamphlets have been developed especially for parents. An example is *Drug Abuse Prevention: A Guide for Parents*, published in 1988. The company must be called for pricing information.

6

Periodicals

COA Review. Rutherford, NJ: Thomas W. Perrin, Inc. (5 Glen Road, Box 190, Rutherford, NJ 07070). 1983- . bimonthly.

The goal of the publishers of this newsletter is to draw attention to the problems of children who grow up in alcoholic families. It is hoped that a network of people and ideas can be built through which these children can receive support. The eight-page publication contains announcements, reviews of new books and films, articles, reports of research, and news.

DIN Newservice. Phoenix, AZ: DIN Publications (Box 21126, Phoenix, AZ 85036-1126). 1893- . bimonthly. $12.00 per year.

This tabloid-format publication was formerly the slick news magazine *Drug Survival News.* The new publication focuses more broadly on "health and behavior" information. It is aimed at a general readership but would appeal to those who are involved with drugs personally or who are tolerant of drug abuse. This publication may be considered controversial.

Drug Enforcement. Washington, D.C.: Drug Enforcement Administration, U.S. Department of Justice (1405 I Street, NW, Washington, D.C. 20537). 1970- . monthly. Three years free.

This publication continues the *BNDD Bulletin.* It is now available online. Articles of miscellaneous matters of drug enforcement are presented with many photographs, some in color. There is often a section on notable cases and also photographs and descriptions of persons wanted by the Drug Enforcement Administration. There have been a number of special issues.

Drugs and Drug Abuse Education Newsletter. Washington, D.C.: Editorial Resources, Inc. (Box 21129, Washington, D.C. 20009, Subscription Address: Box 21133, Washington, D.C. 20009). 1970- . monthly. $53.00 per year.

Formerly called *Washington Drug Review*, this publication merged with and incorporated *Drugs and Drug Abuse Education News* in October 1976. The newsletter provides key information from Washington on treatment and research phases of the drug abuse field. News of federal activities, trends, policies, and funding in the field is reported.

Focus on Family and Chemical Dependence. Pompano Beach, FL: U.S. Journal of Drug and Alcohol Dependency, Inc. 1978- . bimonthly. $22.00.

Formerly called *Focus on Alcohol and Drug Issues*, this attractive slick-paper publication is now geared entirely to family issues resulting from alcohol and drug abuse. Children of alcoholics is a major area of emphasis.

The Journal. Toronto: Addiction Research Foundation (33 Russell St., Toronto, Ontario, Canada M55 2S1). 1972- . monthly. Canada $16.00 per year, U.S. $24.00 per year.

This tabloid-sized publication is designed to familiarize professionals and other interested persons with recent developments in the substance abuse field. It reports and interprets news in the areas of research, treatment, education, enforcement, and social policy from around the world. Emphasis is on Canada and the U.S., however. Included are reviews of books and audiovisual materials. The publication is well done and has a good deal of popular appeal. The reviews of audiovisual materials are particularly valuable for those seeking such information.

Journal of Alcohol and Drug Education. Lansing, MI: Alcohol and Drug Problems Association of North America (c/o MICAP, Box 10212, Lansing, MI 48901). About 1955- . Three times per year. $25.00 to nonmembers, $20.00 for members per year.

Formerly called *Journal of Alcohol Education*, this periodical serves as a forum for various educational philosophies and provides a reference resource for educators on teaching materials, procedures, and techniques. In addition, it reports on new programs on substance abuse education for the community, the church, and the family. Each year, one issue provides an annotated bibliography of educational materials prepared by the Alcohol Education Section of the Information Services Division of the Rutgers Center of Alcohol Studies.

Journal of Drug Education. Farmingdale, NY: Baywood Publishing Co. (120 Marine St., Box D, Farmingdale, NY 11735). 1971- . quarterly. $27.00 to individuals, $75.00 to institutions per year.

Covering the physiological, psychological, pharmacological, legal, and social aspects of drug use, this journal provides information and data of importance on organized educational drug programs. Subjects dealt with include the role of the educator in drug education; innovations in drug education; school and community drug education programs; drug research information; and drug education as applied to business and industry, law enforcement, the clergy, military, and other areas sensitive to the misuse of drugs.

The periodical is indexed in several major references, including *Psychological Abstracts, Excerpta Medica, Biological Abstracts*, and *Abstracts on Criminology and Penology.*

Journal on Psychoactive Drugs: A Multidisciplinary Forum. San Francisco: Haight-Ashbury Publications (409 Clayton St., San Francisco, CA 94117). 1967- . quarterly. $50.00 per year to individuals, $70.00 per year to institutions.

Formerly called the *Journal of Psychedelic Drugs*, the goal of this journal when established was said to be to provide a method of dissemination of honest, objective drug information and to alert workers in the field to the rapidly changing drug abuse pattern that developed in the Haight-Ashbury district of San Francisco and spread to other parts of the country. In later issues emphasis was on special themes and what was called the "politics of drug abuse." More recently still, the increasing research on drug abuse encouraged the expansion of the journal, and there have been a number of theme issues, for instance one on sexological aspects of substance use and abuse and one on cocaine smoking. A wide variety of articles are accepted for publication. These are critical and historical reviews, theoretical analyses, speculative papers with a systematic focus, and a limited number of reports of research. Overly technical articles, however, are usually not published. The journal has gained respectability since its inception; the editorial review board includes some noted authorities in the field.

PharmChem Newsletter. Menlo Park, CA: PharmChem Laboratories (3925 Bohannon Drive, Menlo Park, CA 94025). 1972- . bimonthly. $25.00 per year.

Issues of this publication of ten to twelve pages usually contain a few short articles about drugs of abuse with the intention of supplying factual information. It is a useful guide to "street" drug trends as the emphasis is on determining and publishing the actual content of "street" drugs. Long lists are published giving the following: alleged content, actual content, description, origin (city), date, and street price. An objective of the laboratory is to provide at a nominal cost, and on an anonymous basis, an analysis service on illicit drugs. A similar service is offered by *Street Pharmacologist* cited below. An analysis service of this kind is useful to a variety of clientele, including street drug users themselves, parents, hospitals, medical professionals, and perhaps drug enforcement personnel.

Street Pharmacologist. Miami, FL: Up Front, Inc. (5701 Biscayne Blvd., Ste. 602, Miami, FL 33137). 1978- . monthly. $25.00 per year.

The subtitle of this periodical is "Your Independent Drug Information Center." It contains news, comments, and articles related to drugs of abuse and their effects. In addition, it publishes analysis results of sample substances (presumably illicit "street" drugs) sent to the journal. In tabular form, the substances are described physically, with alleged contents, actual contents, and origin of the samples. Readers are advised that they may have a substance analyzed if they will wrap a small sample of it and send $15 to an address indicated. Later, they may call anonymously and obtain the results.

The aim of the publication is said to be "to collect and share information about drugs and health in ways to minimize problems people encounter in our chemically oriented society." Many of the contributors to the publications evidently have first-hand experience with drug abuse.

Substance Abuse Report. New York: Pace Publications (443 Park Avenue So., New York, NY 10016). 1970- . monthly. $95.00 per year.

The title of this newsletter was formerly *Addiction and Drug Abuse Report*. It then became *Addiction and Substance Abuse Report*. It treats the management of substance abusers, trends in substance abuse, and what schools, factories, businesses, hospitals, or service agencies are doing about them. Included also are how to spot substance abuse and how to handle it, treat it, or live with it.

U.S. Journal of Drug and Alcohol Dependence. Pompano Beach, FL: U.S. Journal of Drug and Alcohol Dependence, Inc. (1721 Blount Rd., Ste. 1, Pompano Beach, FL 33069). 1977- . monthly. $29.00 per year.

This tabloid-sized periodical is similar to *The Journal* issued by the Addiction Research Foundation. It covers news and current concerns, social and political, on all aspects of drug and alcohol abuse. It also provides coverage of conferences, interviews with leaders in the field, and reports on federal legislative news as it relates to funding, regulations, and programming. Comments on advances in research, treatment development, preventive education, and enforcement policies are included.

Appendix A

Substance Abuse Media Evaluation Form

MEDIA EVALUATION FORM

	Type of Media:
	Requested for Preview by:
Title:	
Author/Producer:	Curriculum Area:
Publisher/Company:	Grade Level:
Source:	Subject:
Copyright Date:	
Price:	
Physical Description (length, frames, units, etc.):	
Support Materials Include:	Supports Teaching Method:
	Supports Learning Method:
	Other Uses:
Special Equipment Needed:	
Synopsis:	
______Recommended	Reviewed in:
Priority for Purchase______	Reviewed by teachers:
Please order______copies.	Reviewed by students:

Please place additional comments on reverse.

Bibliography of other materials on this subject is attached.

Appendix B

Library of Congress Key Headings

Term	Narrower Terms	Broader Terms
Alcohol	Alcoholic beverages	
–Law and Legislation		
–Physiological effect		Temperance
	Alcohol–Toxicology	
	Drinking and airplane accidents	
	Drinking and traffic accidents	
Alcohol in the body	Blood alcohol	Biological chemistry
Alcoholics	Children of alcoholics	Alcoholism
	Social work with alcoholics	
–Family relationships		
–Rehabilitation		
Alcoholism	Alcoholics	Substance abuse
	Skid row	Temperance
–Prevention		
–Psychological aspects		
–Religious aspects		
–Study and Teaching		
Alcoholism and Crime	Crime and Criminals	

Alcoholism counseling		
Alcoholism in pregnancy		
Drug abuse	Amphetamine abuse	Substance abuse
	Drugs and sex	
	Hallucinogenic drugs	
	Marihuana	
	Medication abuse	
	Narcotic habit	
	Narcotics dealers	
—Prevention		
—Social aspects		
—Study and teaching		
—Treatment		
Drug abuse and crime		
Drug abuse counseling		
Drug abuse in pregnancy		
Drug abuse surveys		
Drug-alcohol interactions		
Drug testing		Medical screening
Drug withdrawal symptoms		
Drugs		
—Psychological effect		
Drugs and Employment		
Drugs and Sex		
Smoking	Cigarette habit	Oral habits
	Cigarette smokers	Tobacco
	Cigarettes	
	Passive smoking	
—Law and Legislation		
Substance abuse	Aerosol sniffing	Crimes without victims
	Alcoholism	
	Caffeine habit	
	Drug abuse	
	Solvent abuse	
	Tobacco habit	

Appendix C

Sample Search Strategy: BRS*

The search strategy shown below is an example of using Boolean logic to define the perimeters of the search. A sample of the output of the search follows reproducing five entries from the total available. The output from the search required fifty-one pages to print.

1. Drug-Abuse.de
2. 1 and Sedatives.de
3. 2 and Valium
4. Drug-use or

1. Tobacco.de
2. 1 and Smoking.de
3. 2 and Special-health-problems.de

---

*BRS originally stood for Bibliographic Retrieval Service. At this time, the service is called BRS and no longer carries the full title.

```
SUBSTANCE ABUSE                                    6907 DOCUMENTS
DRUG                                               5900 DOCUMENTS
DRUGS                                              1908 DOCUMENTS

RESULT               3342 DOCUMENTS
4   :  substance adj abuse

SUBSTANCE                                          1296 DOCUMENTS
ABUSE                                              6143 DOCUMENTS

RESULT               447 DOCUMENTS
5   :  4 and drug $1

SUBSTANCE ADJ ABUSE                                 477 DOCUMENTS
DRUG                                               5900 DOCUMENTS
DRUGS                                              1909 DOCUMENTS

RESULT               357 DOCUMENTS
6  :  4 and alcohol

SUBSTANCE ADJ ABUSE                                 477 DOCUMENTS
ALCP  OHOL                                    SEARCH TERM NOT FOUND

RESULT                 0 DOCUMENTS
7  :  4 and alcohol

SUBSTANCE ADJ ABUSE                                 477 DOCUMENTS
ALCOHOL                                            2423 DOCUMENTS

RESULT               157 DOCUMENTS
8  :  ..P 7F2/doc-all

USING SEARCH STATEMENT NUMBER 007.
D003  RE-ENTER PARAGRAPH SELECTION... INVALID CODE WAS DOO-ALL  :
..p 7 42/ooc=all

     1
AN  EJ372681.
AU  Bolton, Suzanne.
TI  Youth at Risk:  An Ounce of Prevention.
SO  Update on Law-Related Education; v12 n2 p10-12 Spr 1988.88.
LG  EN..
IS  CNJOCT88.
CH  S0517999.
PT  080; 052; 120.
YR  88.
MJ  Curricoulum-Dcvclopmcnt.  Deliquency-Prevention.
```

Educational-Objectives. Relevance-Education.
School-Responsibility. School Role.
MN Alcohol-Education. Drug-Education. Elementary-Education.
Futures-of-Society. Junior-High Schools. Law-Related-Education.
Peer-Influence.

2
AN EJ372124.
AU Johnson, John L.
TI The Challenge of Substance Abuse.
SO Teaching Exceptional Children; v20 n p.29-31 Sum 1988.88.
LG EN..
IS CIJOCT88.
CH EC202856.
PT 080; 055.
AV UMI.
YR 88.
MJ Alcoholism. Disabilities. Drug-Abuse.
MN Ability-Identification. Elementary-secondary-education
Handicap-Identification. High-risk-students.
Psychoeducational-methods. Student-characteristics.
Student-Evaluation.
ID IDENTIFIERS: Substance Abuse. TARGET AUDIENCE: Practitioners.

3
AN EJ370215.
AU Moore, David D.
TI "Growing Healthy": An Effective Substance Abuse Prevention Program.
SO Educational Leadership; v45 n6 p13 Mar 1988.88.
LG EN..
IS CIJSEP88.
CH EA522126.
PT 080; 141.
AV UMI.
YR 88.
MJ Alcoholism. Drug-Abuse. Health-Education. Prevention.
Teacher-Education.
MN Elementary-Secondary-Education.

4
AN EJ370213.
AU Horton, Lowell.
TI The Education of Most Worth: Preventing Drug and Alcohol Abuse.
SO Educational Leadership; v45 n6 p4-8 Mar 1988. 88.

LG EN..
IS CIJSEP88.
CH EA522124.
PT 000; 141.
AV UMI.
YR 88.
MJ Adolescents. Alcohol-Education. Drinking. Drug-Abuse. Prevention.
MN Secondary-Education.

5
AN EJ369925
AU Schinke, Steven P.; and Others.
TI Preventing Substance Abuse among American-Indian Adolescents: A Bicultural Competence Skills Approach.
SO Journal of Counseling Psychology; v35 n1 p87-90 Jan 1988.88.
LG EN.
IS CIJSEP88.
CH CG533830.
PT 080; 140; 143.
AV UMI.
YR 88
MJ Adolescents. Alcoholism. American-Indians. Drug-Abuse. Prevention. Smoking.
MN Attitudes. Biculturalism. Competence. Interpersonal-Competence. Knowledge-Level. Program-Effectiveness.

Appendix D

Suggested Databases to Search for Substance Abuse Information*

Database	Label	Producer	Description
Alcohol Information Clinicians and Educators	Cork	Project Cork Institute, Dartmouth Medical School	Alcohol & alcoholism issues
Alcohol & Alcohol Problems Science	ETOH	National Institute on Alcohol Abuse & Alcoholism	Alcohol & related scientific references
Combined Health Information Database	CHID	Combined Health Information Database	Health education & patient-oriented health care information
Comprehensive Care Medical Library	CCML	Major Medical Publishers	Full Text of Medical Textbooks and Journals

*The practice databases provide for less expensive searching time for educators to use in training sessions. A special instructor's password is usually assigned.

CCML Journal Subset	JOUR	Major Medical Publishers	Journal subset of CCML
CCML Book Subset	MEDB	Major Medical Publishers	Textbook subset of CCML
Consumer Drug Information Database	CDIF	American Society of Hospital Pharmacists	Full-text consumer drug information
Current Contents Search	CCON	Institute for Scientific Information	Applied sciences, life sciences, agriculture, and medicine
Current Contents Search: Clinical Medicine	CLIN	Institute for Scientific Information	Clinical practice and medicine
Current Contents Search: Social and Behavioral Sciences	BEHA	Institute for Scientific Information	Social and behavioral sciences
Diogenes	DIOG	Diogenes	Regulatory information for the health care industry
Drug Info./Alcohol Use-Abuse (Merged)	DRUG	University of Minnesota College of Pharmacy	Drug abuse and alcoholism
Drug Info.	DRSC	University of Minnesota College of Pharmacy	Drug abuse
Alcohol Use-Abuse	HAZE	University of Minnesota College of Pharmacy	Alcoholism
Drug Information Full Text	DIFT	American Society of Hospital Pharmacists	Full-text information on current and investigational drugs

Embase Drug Information	EMDR	Elsevier Science Publishers	Pharmaceutical subset of EMBASE
ERIC (Educational Resources Information Center)	ERIC	National Institute of Education	Education
Federal Register Abstracts	FREG	National Standards Association	Abstracts to the Federal Register
Health Industry Research Reports	HIRR	JA Micropublishing, Inc.	Health industry subset of CIRR
Index to U.S. Government Periodicals	GOVT	Infordata International, Inc.	Indexes of U.S. government periodicals
International Pharmaceutical Abstracts	IPAB	American Society Hospital Pharmacists	Pharmaceutical and drug-related information
Journal Watch	JWAT	Medical Publishing Group	Medical literature news service
Legal Resource	LAWS	Information Access Co.	Legal reviews, journals
Magazine Index	MAGS	Information Access Co.	General-interest magazines
Magazine ASAP III	MSAP	Information Access Co.	Full-text magazine articles

Medical & Psychological Previews	PREV	BRS Information Technologies	Current awareness for medical and psychology journals
Medical Science Research Database	IRCS	Medical Science Research	Full-text biomedical research
Medline and Backfiles Medline (Merged)	MESB MESH MESZ	National Library of Medicine (NLM)	Medicine, nursing, dentistry
Merck Index	MRCK	Merck & Co.	Chemicals, drugs and substances of biological importance
New England Journal of Medicine	NEJM	Massachusetts Medical Society	Full text of NEJM (subset of CCML)
NTIS Bibliographic Database	NTIS	National Technical Information Service	Government reports, all areas
PAIS International	PAIS	Public Affairs Information Service	Public policy issues
Pharmaceutical News Index	PNII	UMI/Data Courier	Pharmaceutical Industry News
Popular Magazine Review Online	PMRO	Ebsco Industries Inc.	Index to popular U.S. magazines

Psycalert	PSAL	American Psychological Association	Current psychological literature
Psycinfo	PSYC	American Psychological Association	Psychology
REHABATA	NRIC	National Rehabilitation Information Center	Rehabilitation literature
Scientific American Medicine	SAMM	Scientific American, Inc.	Current information on internal medicine
Social Planning/Policy & Development Abstracts	SPDA	Sociological Abstracts	Social welfare policy & development
Social SCISEARCH	SSCI	Institute for Scientific Information	Social sciences
Social Work Abstracts	SWAB	National Association for Social Workers	Social work, related fields
Sociological Abstracts & Social Planning/Policy & Development Abstracts/ International Review of Publications in Sociology	SOCZ	Sociological Abstracts	Sociology, social policy, and related disciplines
Sociological Abstracts	SOCA	Sociological Abstracts	Sociology and related disciplines
Sport Database	SFDB	Sport Information Resource Center	Sport, fitness, recreation, sports medicine

PRACTICE DATABASES

Practice Complete Text Journals	PCTJ	Major Medical Publishers	Practice journal subset of CCML
Practice Journals	PMED	National Library of Medicine	Practice subset of MEDLINE
Social SCISEARCH Practice	SSCP	Institute for Scientific Information	Practice subset of social SCISEARCH
Embase Practice	EMET	Elsevier Science Publishers	Practice subset of EMBASE

Appendix E

Why Do Adolescents Use Substances (Drugs/Alcohol)?

"Why Do Adolescents Use Substances (Drugs/Alcohol)?"
Zigmond A. Kozicki*
The Journal of Alcohol and Drug Education
1986

WHAT IS ADOLESCENCE?

Adolescence is a period of development during which the young person, no longer a child and more or less physiologically mature, must gradually loosen the ties which have bound him/her to the home and to his/her parents. His/her social, intellectual and sexual interests expand and broaden. He/she must now begin to establish him/herself as an independent human being.

It is a period of transition from childhood to adulthood. It is a period of time when young people search for their identity as an adult. It is a time of intense feelings and emotions. In modern western society, it is typically the human developmental period between the ages of 12 and 18 years of age. As of 1980, there were approximately 21 million adolescents ("U.S. Census, News Focus 1981," *Newsweek* v.5) in the United States.

During this time young people experience role-confusion and search for meaning. Young people often use substances (alcohol and drugs) as part of the process of seeking answers to their numerous questions about their role and self-identity. Substances are used ritually and habitually by young people to intensify their strong need to find themselves and their role in the adult world.

---

*Reprinted with permission from *The Journal of Alcohol and Drug Education*. Vol. 32, no. 1 (1986).

STATISTICS ABOUT ADOLESCENT SUBSTANCE USE

Data about substance use in young people points out that there has been a significant increase since the 1960's in terms of problems with substance use. For example, in the thirteen years between 1960 through 1973, arrests for drug offenses increased by 4.673.3% for youngsters under the age of 18 years (*Uniform Crime Reports*, 1973, pp. 124-125). Statistics point out that males typically have a higher incidence of drug abuse than females by a ratio of about 2 to 1. Adolescent drug users are also inclined to use more than one drug (Johnston, 1973). Substance usage by adolescents ... "appears to be associated with pessimism, unhappiness, boredom, aggressiveness, frustration, impulsiveness, distrust, cynicism, irresponsibility, inflexibility, and dissatisfaction...." Correlations exist between substance use and ... "antisocial or delinquent behavior...." Heavier consumption of substances has been linked to ... "precocious sexual behavior, poor school performance, problem behavior in the classroom, number of classes cut from school, problems within the family, and higher dropout rates...." (*Alcohol and Health*, January 1981).

SUBSTANCE ABUSE

Substance abuse refers to an excessive use of one or more chemical substances that are considered harmful to the person's health and personal adjustment or to society. This paper recognizes eight major drug groups that continue to find frequent usage by adolescents. They are: heroin, marijuana, amphetamines, barbiturates, methaqualone, tranquilizers, alcohol and tobacco.

REASONS ADOLESCENTS USE SUBSTANCES

Substances are taken to achieve an unusual mood or to obliterate unpleasurable and uncomfortable feelings. Substances are stimuli which affect the user's capacity to feel excitement. In its most elementary sense, excitement provides the basis for distress and delight in all people. It is for this reason that substance usage can be both a negative and a positive experience for people.

When it is a negative experience, people feel anger, fear and disgust. When it is a positive experience, people are led to feel elation and affection. People will use substances whenever they find that it reinforces and excites them. For some people, negative emotions reinforce; in others, positive emotions reinforce. Adolescents have a strong compulsion for excitement. Substance use is one stimuli which increases the adolescent's capacity to feel excitement. Adolescents, like all people, use substances to reach excitement irregardless of whether it is negative or positive emotional experience.

LEARNING AND DEVELOPMENT

Learning is the process by which environmental forces bring about lasting changes in behavior through practice (Knopf, I.J., *Child Psychopathology*,

1979). All people learn how to be substance users and abusers. Substance abuse develops in people just as any other behavior would. Human development, however, is a process that is affected by numerous factors.

It is recognized that the following factors affect human development. These include biology, which encompasses heredity and congenital effects; maturation, which includes both changes in anatomical and physiological development in a human being; temperament, which is each individual's distinctive behavioral style; prenatal/postnatal care; drugs and other chemicals ingested by the human organism; and nutrition, both excessive and inadequate consumption of food affects development.

There are also socio-psychological factors which affect human development. A person's race, social class, cultural context, family, school, peer relationships, early neonatal experiences, influences by mother and father and significant others, all affect human development. Other factors to consider include the learning potential of a person and the person's actual intellectual quotient (Knopf, I.J. *Child Psychopathology*, 1979).

In each human organism, the potential to be a substance abuser exists. In some, it is realized. For others, it is not. No doubt, the numerous factors affecting human development play a significant role in shaping some individuals to be substance abusers while others do not experience this particular behavior. Researchers are finding that some factors can be identified as chief contributors towards substance abuse behavior.

PARENTAL INFLUENCE

The single most significant influence on the development of a human organism is the parents. It has been pointed out by researchers (Mercer, G. William, and Kohn, P.M., 1980) that parents' child-rearing practices produce within the child a personality that shapes attitudes toward the use of drugs, which in turn affects the child's use of marijuana, alcohol and tobacco. Their findings pointed out that authoritarian parents have a strong influence on use pattern of adolescents. It is also noted that parents who were heavy users or abstainers had the greatest number of children with substance abuse problems (Fort, J., 1973). It would appear that the combination of authoritarian parenting style and heavy use or abstinence by parents promotes substance abuse in children.

When one looks at the profile of an adolescent substance abuser, it appears that the effects of authoritarian and inadequate modeling of substance use produces salient behaviors in the adolescent. These include a need to be more dominant, radical attitudes, aggressiveness, self-indulgence, less inhibition and more extroversion (Kurg, S.E., and Henry, T. J., 1976). Current estimates are that at least 12 million children in the United States are in the high-risk group in terms of either developing or having started to develop problems using substances. It is estimated that approximately 5% of these children are receiving help (*Alcohol and Health*, January 1981).

OTHER REASONS FOR ADOLESCENTS' SUBSTANCE USE

There are three apparent explanations for substance use in adolescents that have received popular acceptance. It is felt that adolescents use substances:

1. as a means to be accepted by their peers,
2. in order to demonstrate rebellion against society and/or parents,
3. as a method to cope with personality problems.

FACTS ABOUT SUBSTANCE USERS

Heroin

It is estimated that there are approximately 250 thousand active addicts in the United States who live primarily in impoverished areas and are predominantly male (85%) (Wald and Hutt, 1972). Researchers have found that addicts are more likely to have experienced an unhappy childhood, harsh physical punishment and little parental concern for their school work, sexual conduct, careers, or choice of friends (Milkman and Frosch, 1973). It is estimated that death from heroin usage occurs in 25% of the addicts (Eldefonso, 1972).

Marijuana

It is estimated from 3-20% of Americans are daily users of marijuana. One out of six youngsters, age 12 through 17 years, use it regularly (*U.S. National Survey on Drug Use*, 1979). The profile of the marijuana user is that they are liberal, non-religious, cigarette smokers, who have parents who used substances. It was also found that they were not likely to be involved in criminal acts when other drugs were not used (Goode, E., 1975).

Amphetamines

Until the last few years, approximately 12 million pills of this stimulant is legally produced by pharmaceutical houses each year in the United States (Grinspoon and Hedblom, 1975). The heaviest abusers of amphetamines are adolescents who may have started use for weight control or to stay awake for academic assignments. It is known that people who use amphetamines like to do so to maintain a posture of active confrontation with their environment (Milkman and Frosch, 1973).

Barbiturates

Approximately 34 doses of this sedative, for each person over the age of 10 years of age, is being supplied each year by both legal and illegal channels in the United States (Bates and Crowther, 1973). Adolescents like to use barbiturates to get down, relax and reduce tension.

Methaqualone

A powerful depressant, sold legitimately and prescribed by physicians as a sedative. In 1981, it is estimated that a billion tablets were consumed in the United States (Carper, J., 1981). Its effects on the human nervous system is similar to alcohol. It is, however, a more powerful concentrated depressant which young people find to be more convenient and less confiscatable than liquor. Methaqualone, like all pill medication, are easy to conceal from parents, teachers, the police, etc.

Tranquilizers

A sedative hypnotic group of drugs used primarily to reduce anxiety and tension. They are the most widely-prescribed drugs in the United States. It is estimated that approximately 20% of the people in the United States use tranquilizers (Urleuth, E., Butler, M., Lipman, S., 1978). Adolescents find that the drug's availability makes its usage popular.

Alcohol

Alcohol is the most popular depressant drug used in the United States. It is estimated that 2.7 gallons per year of alcohol (ethanol) per person 14 years of age and older is consumed in the United States. It is estimated that one ounce of ethanol equals two drinks. In the United States, present consumption now averages about one ounce of ethanol each day for each person 14 years of age and older (Clark and Midanik, 1979). Overall consumption of alcohol in the United States has increased since 1934 (Distilled Spirits Council of the United States, 1978 and U.S. Department of Health, Education and Welfare, 1978, 1980). It is estimated that approximately 28% of high school students use alcohol once a week or more often (Rachal, 1978).

All drinking problems show their highest prevalence in younger adults. With increasing age the number of abstainers rises. Males are more strongly influenced by their external environment toward alcohol usage. Women, on the other hand, are more strongly influenced by their feelings of alienation and/or maladjustment (Cahalan, 1970).

Tobacco

In 1980, 630 billion cigarettes were consumed in the United States by 53 million users (*Time*, March 8, 1982). Approximately 10.7% of teen-age boys and 12.7% of teen-age girls smoke cigarettes (American Cancer Society, *View of Smoking*, 1981). "The age of greatest susceptibility to becoming a regular smoker is age 12" (Matarazzo, J.D., 1982). Today, 37% of men and 29% of women use tobacco regularly. Twenty percent of high school seniors smoked daily in 1981 (*Time*, March 8, 1982).

Environmental Influence on Substance Use

Substance use and subsequent abuse is largely determined by: (1) resources available for use, (2) the activities competing for those resources, and (3) the cost associated with the use (Storm and Cutler, 1975). Three major themes are stressed by ad agency campaigns to promote substance use. These include the promotion of the belief that sexual pleasure and conquest, youthfulness and general happiness or comfort will be reached by using the substance being promoted (Fort, J., 1973).

Summary

The period of adolescence, ages 12 through 18, is a difficult time of role confusion for 21 million people. Substance use among this group of people has increased dramatically since 1960. Males typically have a higher incidence of substance abuse problems. Adolescents are inclined to use more than one drug. Numerous behavioral problems are associated with substance abuse. Substance use and its subsequent abuse is a learned process. Developmental factors affect this learning process. Parental influence significantly influences substance use and abuse patterns in adolescents. Adolescents use substances because of peer pressure, to express their individuality through rebellion, as a method of coping with personality conflicts and in order to become excited. Heroin, marijuana, amphetamines, barbiturates, methaqualone, tranquilizers, alcohol and tobacco are among the most popular drugs used by adolescents. The resources available for use of substances overwhelmingly promote substance use by adolescents.

REFERENCES

Alcohol and Health, 4th Special Report to the U.S. Congress. Secretary of Health and Human Services, January, 1981. p. 18.

American Cancer Society, "View of Smoking," *Fewer Smoking* 1981.

Bates, W., and B. Crowther. *Drugs: Causes, Circumstances, and Effects of Their Use.* Morristown, New Jersey: General Learning Press, 1973.

Cahalan, D. *Problem Drinkers.* San Francisco: Jossey-Bass, Inc., Publishers, 1970.

Carper, J. "Deadlier Than Heroin," *Readers Digest*, May 1982.

Clark, W. B., Midanik, L. "Alcohol Use and Alcohol Problems Among U.S. Adults In: N.I.A.A.A." *Alcohol Consumption and Related Problems*, Rockville, MD 1981.

Distilled Spirits Council of the United States (DISCUS), "Apparent Consumption of Distilled Spirits by Months and by States, 1977," Washington, D.C. *DISCUS,* 1978.

Eldefonso, E. *Youth Problems and Law Enforcement*, Wiley, 1983.

Erickson, L. G. and Cramer, J.A. "Smoking Behavior Development and Modification," *Journal of Applied Social Psychology*, 1976 (Oct.-Dec.) Vol. 6(4), 369-386.

Fort, J. *Alcohol Our Biggest Drug Problem*, McGraw Hill, 1973.

Goode, E. "Sociological Aspects of Marijuana Use." *Contemporary Drug Problems*, 1975 (Win), Vol. 4(4), 397-445.

Grinspoon, L. and P. Hedblom. *The Speed Culture: Amphetamine Use and Abuse in America*, Cambridge, Massachusetts: Harvard University Press, 1975.

Halikas, J. A. and J. D. Rimmer. "Predictions of Multiple Drug Abuse," *Archives of General Psychiatry*, 1974, 31, 414-418.

Johnston, L. "Drugs and American Youth: A Report from the Youth in Transition Project," Ann Arbor, Michigan: Institute for Social Research, University of Michigan, 1973.

Knopf, J. J. *Child Psychopathology*, Englewood Cliffs, New Jersey: Prentice-Hall, Inc., 1979, p. 77 and pp. 54-99.

Krug, S. E. and Henry, T. J. "Personality, Motivation, and the Adolescent Drug Use Patterns." *School Psychology Digest*, 1976, (Spr), Vol. 5(2), 17-23.

Matarazzo, J. D. "Behavioral Health's Challenge to Academic, Scientific, and Professional Psychology." *American Psychologist*, Vol. 37, Jan. 82, No. 1.

Mercer, G. W. and Kohn, P. M. "Child-rearing Factors, Authoritarianism, Drug Use Attitudes, and the Adolescent Drug Use." *Journal of Genetic Psychology*, 1980 (Jun), Vol. 135(2), 159-171.

Milkman, H. and W. A. Frosch. "On the Preferential Abuse of Heroin and Amphetamine." *Journal of Nervous and Mental Diseases*, 1973, 156.

Newsweek, "News Focus U.S. Census 1981," Dec., Visual #5.

Rachal, J. V., Maisto, S. A., Guess, L. L., and Hubbard R. L. "Alcohol Use Among Adolescents." In: N.I.A.A.A. *Alcohol Consumption and Related Problems*, Rockville, MD 1981.

Storm, T. and Cutler, R. "Alcohol Consumption and Personal Resources: A General Hypothesis and Some Implications." *Journal of Studies on Alcohol*, 1975, (Jul).

"*Time* Report from the Surgeon General," 4/8/82, Vol. 119, No. 10, p. 72.

U.S. Department of Health, Education and Welfare, *Third Special Report to the U.S. Congress on Alcohol and Health.* E. P. Nobel, ed. DHEW Pub. No. (ADM) 79-832, 1978.

Uniform Crime Reports, Federal Bureau of Investigation. Washington, D.C.: U.S. Government Printing Office, 1973, pp. 124-125.

Urlcuth, E. Butler, M., Lipman, S. "Minor Tranquilizers." *Archives of General Psychiatry*, May, 1978.

Wald, P. M., and P. B. Hurr. *Dealing with Drug Abuse: A Report to the Ford Foundation*. New York: Praeger, 1972.

Appendix F

State Agencies for Further Assistance

The National Association of State Alcohol and Drug Abuse Directors is the national headquarters for information concerning state agencies.

Each state and territory has an official agency for the prevention and treatment of drug abuse and alcohol problems. Contact your state or territory agency or the national association for assistance with matters related to substance abuse.

National Association of State Alcohol and Drug Abuse Directors

440 North Capitol Street NW
Suite 530
Washington, D.C. 20001

Alabama

Division of Mental Illness and Substance Abuse
Community Programs
Department of Mental Health
P.O. Box 3710
Montgomery, AL 36193

Alaska

Office of Alcoholism and Drug Abuse
Dept. of Health and Social Services
Pouch H-05-F
Juneau, AK 99811

Arizona

Office of Comm. Behav. Health
Dept. of Health Services
701 East Jefferson
Suite 400A
Phoenix, AZ 85034

Arkansas

Office on Alcohol and Drug Abuse Prevention
Donaghey Plaza North
Suite 400
P.O. Box 1437
Little Rock, AR 72203-1437

California

Dept. of Alcohol and Drug Programs
111 Capitol Mall
Suite 450
Sacramento, CA 95814

Colorado

Alcohol and Drug Abuse Division
Dept. of Health
4210 East 11th Avenue
Denver, CO 80220

Connecticut

Alcohol and Drug Abuse Commission
999 Asylum Avenue
Hartford, CT 06105

Delaware

Bureau of Alcoholism and Drug Abuse
1901 North DuPont Highway
Newcastle, DE 19720

District of Columbia

Health Planning and Development
1875 Connecticut Ave., N.W.
Suite 836
Washington, DC 20009

Florida

Alcohol and Drug Abuse Program
Dept. of Health and Rehabilitative Services
1317 Winewood Blvd.
Tallahassee, FL 32301

Georgia

Alcohol and Drug Services Section
878 Peachtree Street, N.E.
Suite 318
Atlanta, GA 30309

Hawaii

Alcohol and Drug Abuse Branch
Dept. of Health
P.O. Box 3378
Honolulu, HI 96801

Idaho

Bureau of Substance Abuse and Social Services
Dept. of Health and Welfare
450 West State Street
Boise, ID 83720

Illinois

Dept. of Alcoholism and Substance Abuse
100 West Randolph Street
Suite 5-600
Chicago, IL 60601

Indiana

Div. of Addiction Services
Dept. of Mental Health
117 East Washington Street
Indianapolis, IN 46204

Iowa

Dept. of Public Health
Div. of Substance Abuse and Health Promotion
Lucas State Office Bldg.
Des Moines, IA 50319

Kansas

Alcohol and Drug Abuse Services
2700 West Sixth Street
Biddle Bldg.
Topeka, KS 66606

Kentucky

Division of Substance Abuse
Dept. for Mental Health
Mental Retardation Services
275 East Main Street
Frankfort, KY 40621

Louisiana

Office of Prevention and Recovery from Alcohol and Drug Abuse
2744 B Woodale Boulevard
Baton Rouge, LA 70805

Maine

Office of Alcoholism and Drug Abuse Prevention
Bureau of Rehabilitation
State House Station #11
Augusta, ME 04333

Maryland

State Drug Abuse Administration
201 West Preston Street
Baltimore, MD 21201

Massachusetts

Div. of Substance Abuse Services
150 Tremont Street
Boston, MA 02111

Michigan

Office of Substance Abuse Services
Dept. of Public Health
3423 North Logan Street
P.O. Box 30035
Lansing, MI 48909

Minnesota

Chemical Dependency Program Div.
Dept. of Human Services
Centennial Bldg.
658 Cedar Street
St. Paul, MN 55155

Mississippi

Div. of Alcohol and Drug Abuse
Dept. of Mental Health
State Office Bldg.
1500 Woolfolk
Jackson, MS 39201

Missouri

Div. of Alcohol and Drug Abuse
Dept. of Mental Health
1915 South Ridge Dr.
P.O. Box 687
Jefferson City, MO 65102

Montana

Alcohol and Drug Abuse Div.
Dept. of Institutions
Helena, MT 59601

Nebraska

Division of Alcoholism and Drug Abuse
Dept. of Public Institutions
P.O. Box 94728
Lincoln, NE 68509

Nevada

Bureau of Alcohol and Drug Abuse
Dept. of Human Resources
505 East King Street
Carson City, NV 89710

New Hampshire

Office of Alcohol and Drug Abuse Prevention
Health and Welfare Bldg.
Hazen Drive
Concord, NH 03301

New Jersey

Div. of Alcoholism
129 East Hanover Street
Trenton, NJ 08625

Div. of Narcotic and Drug Abuse Control
129 East Hanover St.
Trenton, NJ 08625

New Mexico

Substance Abuse Bureau
Behavioral Health Services Division
P.O. Box 968
Santa Fe, NM 87504

New York

Div. of Alcohol and Alcohol Abuse
194 Washington Ave.
Albany, NY 12210

Div. of Substance Abuse Services
Executive Park South
P.O. Box 8200
Albany, NY 12203

North Carolina

Alcohol and Drug Abuse Section
Div. of Mental Health and Mental Retardation Services
325 North Salisbury Street
Raleigh, NC 27611

North Dakota

Div. of Alcoholism and Drug Abuse
Dept. of Human Services
State Capitol/Judicial Wing
Bismarck, ND 58505

Ohio

Bureau on Alcohol Abuse and Recovery
Dept. of Health
170 North High street
Columbus, OH 43266-0586

Bureau on Drug Abuse
Dept. of Health
170 North High Street
Columbus, OH 43266-0586

Oklahoma

Alcohol and Drug Programs
Dept. of Mental Health
P.O. Box 53277
Capitol Station
Oklahoma City, OK 73152

Oregon

Office of Alcohol and Drug Abuse Programs
301 Public Service Bldg.
Salem, OR 97310

Pennsylvania

Deputy Secretary for Drug and Alcohol Programs
Dept. of Health
P.O. Box 90
Harrisburg, PA 17108

Rhode Island

Div. of Substance Abuse
Substance Abuse Administration Bldg.
Cranston, RI 02920

South Carolina

Commission on Alcohol and Drug Abuse
3700 Forest Drive
Columbia, SC 29204

South Dakota

Div. of Alcohol and Drug Abuse
523 East Capitol
Pierre, SD 57501

Tennessee

Alcohol and Drug Abuse Services
Dept. of Mental Health and Mental Retardation
706 Church Street
Nashville, TN 37219

Texas

Commission on Alcohol and Drug Abuse
1705 Guadalupe St.
Austin, TX 78701

Utah

Div. of Alcoholism and Drugs
150 West North Temple
Suite 350
P.O. Box 2500
Salt Lake City, UT 84110

Vermont

Office of Alcohol and Drug Abuse Programs
103 South Maine Street
Waterbury, VT 05676

Virginia

Office of Substance Abuse Services
Dept. of Mental Health and Mental Retardation
P.O. Box 1797
109 Governor Street
Richmond, VA 23214

Washington

Bureau of Alcoholism and Substance Abuse
Dept. of Social and Health Services
Mail Stop 0B-44W
Olympia, WA 98504

West Virginia

Div. of Alcohol and Drug Abuse
State Capitol
Room 451
1800 Washington Street, East
Charleston, WV 25305

Wisconsin

Office of Alcohol and Other Drug Abuse
1 West Wilson Street
P.O. Box 7851
Madison, WI 53707

Wyoming

Alcohol and Drug Abuse Programs
Hathaway Building
Cheyenne, WY 82002

Guam

Dept. of Mental Health and Substance Abuse
P.O. Box 8896
Tamuning, GU 96911

Puerto Rico

Dept. of Anti-Addiction Services
Box B-Y, Rio Piedras Station
Rio Piedras, PR 00928

Virgin Islands

Div. of Mental Health, Alcoholism and Drug Dependency
P.O. Box 520
St. Croix, VI 00820

American Samoa

Human Services Clinic
Public Health Services
Alcohol and Drug Programs
LBJ Tropical Medical Center
Pago Pago, AS 96799

Trust Territories

Health Services
Office of the High Commissioner
Saipan, TT 96950

Appendix G

Al-Anon and Alateen Literature Order Blank

LITERATURE ORDER BLANK
FOR AL-ANON AND ALATEEN
CONFERENCE-APPROVED LITERATURE (CAL) AND MATERIALS

See Al-Anon's Catalogs (S-15) and (S-15R) for description and use of the items listed below.

AL-ANON/ALATEEN BOOKS

	CAT. #	PRICE PER	QUAN.	TOTAL COST
AL-ANON FACES ALCOHOLISM 2nd Edition	B-1	$ 6.50		
ALATEEN—HOPE FOR CHILDREN OF ALCOHOLICS	B-3	4.50		
DILEMMA OF THE ALCOHOLIC MARRIAGE	B-4	5.00		
AL-ANON FAMILY GROUPS	B-5	5.50		
ONE DAY AT A TIME IN AL-ANON	B-6	6.00		
LOIS REMEMBERS	B-7	8.50		
AL-ANON'S TWELVE & TWELVE	B-8	5.50		
FORUM FAVORITES Vols. 1 & 2	B-9	6.25		
ALATEEN—a day at a time	B-10	5.00		
AS WE UNDERSTOOD ... Hardcover, with Index	B-11	6.50		
FIRST STEPS: Al-Anon 35 Years of Beginnings	B-12	9.00		
Larger Print ONE DAY AT A TIME IN AL-ANON	B-14	8.00		

Book Discounts: 50¢ per book on quantities of 5 or more in any combination of titles. 25% on orders of 25 or more of ONE Title.

BOOKLETS, PAMPHLETS & LEAFLETS

	CAT. #	PRICE PER	QUAN.	TOTAL COST
Al-Anon IS for Men	P-1	.20		
Al-Anon, You and the Alcoholic	P-2	.30		
Alcoholism, A Merry-Go-Round Named Denial	P-3	.60		
Alcoholism, The Family Disease	P-4	.60		
Alcoholism, The Family Disease *Larger print*	P-4L	1.15		
Blueprint for Progress: 4th Step Inventory	P-5	1.75		
Freedom from Despair	P-6	.15		
Guide for the Family of the Alcoholic	P-7	.30		
Homeward Bound	P-8	.25		
How Can I Help My Children?	P-9	.55		

BOOKLETS, PAMPHLETS & LEAFLETS cont.

	CAT. #	PRICE PER	QUAN.	TOTAL COST
Living With Sobriety	P-49	2.00		
Al-Anon Is For Adult Children of Alcoholics	P-52	[illegible]		
Al-Anon Spoken Here	P-53	.30		
Planting A Seed	P-55	.40		
The Concepts: Al-Anon's Best Kept Secret?	P-57	.60		
Al-Anon Speaks To You The Professional	P-58	.55		
Al-Anon's Twelve Traditions—Illustrated	P-60	.60		
Does She Drink Too Much?	P-62	.50		
Index to Recovery In CAL	P-63	1.15		

MISCELLANEOUS MATERIALS

	CAT. #	PRICE PER	QUAN.	TOTAL COST
Are you Concerned About . . . 50/1.25 A †	M-1	100/2.25		
Al-Anon Basic Program Wallet Card 12/1.00 A †	M-7	100/7.00		
Declaration Card "Let it Begin..." 20/1.00A †	M-8	100/5.00		
Just For Today, Al-Anon Wallet Card 25/1.00A †	M-10	100/4.00		
Just For Today, Al-Anon Bookmark 12/1.00A †	M-12	100/7.00		
Logos, Al-Anon blue †	M-14	100/2.00		
Logos, Alateen red †	M-15	100/2.00		
"You Can Render. . ." 25/1.00A †	M-19	100/4.00		
Serenity Prayer Card 12/1.00 A	M-26	100/7.00		
FORUM Binder	M-28	5.00		
Al-Anon Spoken Here Door Hang (Al-Anon)	M-39	1.00		
Al-Anon Spoken Here Door Hang (Alateen)	M-40	1.00		
Al-Anon/Alateen Is & Is Not Bookmark †	M-44	20/1.00		
Banners: Al-Anon's Steps & Traditions (vinyl)	M-45	20.00		

Lois' Story	P-11	.30		
Purpose and Suggestions	P-13	.20		
So You Love An Alcoholic	P-14	.20		
Three Views of Al-Anon	P-15	.25		
To the Mother and Father of an Alcoholic	P-16	.60		
Twelve Steps and Traditions	P-17	.60		
What Do You Do About the Alcoholic's Drinking?	P-19	.25		
What's Next? Asks the Husband	P-20	.40	DISCONTINUED	
Al-Anon and Alateen Groups At Work	P-24	1.15		
Digest of Al-Anon/Alateen Policies	P-25	1.15		
Twelve Concepts of Service	P-26	1.15		
World Service Handbook	P-27	1.15		
All 4 Service Manuals	Set	4.00		
Binder for Service Manuals	M-31	3.50		
Sponsorship, What It's All About	P-31	.30		
This is Al-Anon	P-32	.30		
Why is Al-Anon Anonymous?	P-33	.30		
Al-Anon and Professionals	P-34	.50		
Why CAL?	P-35	Free		
Al-Anon Fact File	P-36	.45		
Al-Anon Family Treatment Tool	P-37	.20		
Pebble in the Pond **Revised**	P-42	2.00		
What's "Drunk," Mama?	P-44	1.25		
The Al-Anon Focus	P-45	.20		
World Service Conference Summary (Current)	P-46	1.00		
Al-Anon Sharings From Adult Children	P-47	.60		
Understanding Ourselves & Alcoholism	P-48	.20		

COLUMN A TOTAL

POSTERS

Poster 11 × 14″ printed with illus. Woman .25 A †		M-22	5/1.00		
Miniposter 5½ × 7″ Woman .10 A †		M-22s	3/.25		
Poster 11 × 14″ printed with illus. Man .25 A †		M-23	5/1.00		
Miniposter 5½ × 7″ Man .10 A †		M-23s	3/.25		
Poster 11 × 14″ printed with illus. Teens .25 A †		M-24	5/1.00		
Miniposter 5½ × 7″ Teens .10A†		M-24s	3/.25		
Poster, 4-Color 17 × 22″ Family		M-32	1.50		
Poster, 4-Color 8½ × 11″ Family		M-33	1.00		
Poster 4-Color 6½ × 8½″ Family †		M-34	3/1.00		
Poster "You Don't Have To Drink . . ." 11 × 14″		M-35	.25		
Poster "You Don't Have To Drink..." 6⅝ × 8½″ 5/.50 A †		M-36	.15		
Easel Board 4-color 17 × 22″ Family		M-37	10.00		
Table Display "Alcoholism Can Tear A Family Apart" with Pocket filled with 50 (M-1) leaflets (10 or more $2.50 each) A		M-38	3.00		
Posters Is Alcohol A Problem In Your Family?	English 11 × 14″	M-41	4/1.00		
Alateen poster	English 6⅝ × 8½″	M-41s	5/1.00		
	Spanish 11 × 14″	SM-41	4/1.00		
	Spanish 6⅝ × 8½″	SM-41s	5/1.00		

COLUMN B TOTAL

SUPPLEMENTARY MATERIALS

	CAT. #	PRICE PER	QUAN.	TOTAL COST
Information for the Newcomer	S-4	.15		
Questionnaire for Step 4 Al-Anon	S-5	.15		
Table Anonymity Card	S-9	.30		
Al-Anon, Is It For You? 20 Questions †	S-17	100/2.00		
Detachment 50/1.00A †	S-19	100/2.00		
Getting in Touch With Al-Anon 10/1.50A Revised Information Service Listings †	S-23	.25		
Al-Anon Spoken Here Table Tent Card	S-24	.45		
Did You Grow Up With a Problem Drinker? 20 Questions †	S-25	100/2.00		
Who Are The Members of Al-Anon and Alateen?	S-29	.20		

KITS/PACKETS

P.I. Discount Package—$16.60 value	K-4	13.00		
Sampler: Al-Anon/Alateen Literature	K-8	15.00		
Institutions Discount Package —88 pieces	K-9	7.50		
Newcomers' Packet	K-10	1.25		
Labor-Management Packet— Al-Anon As A Resource	K-11	.50		
Al-Anon Spoken Here Kit (check one) ☐ Al-Anon ☐ Alateen A 10 pamphlets, 1 table card, 1 door hang	K-14	3.00		
Combined Service Workbook	K-17	12.00		
Media Kit	K-19	2.00		
Adult Children of Alcoholics Newcomer's Packet NEW	K-21	1.75		

ORDER BLANKS & CATALOG

Supplementary Materials, Guidelines, Service Aids and Reprints	S-11	Free		
Translated Material	S-13	Free		
Material for the Visually Impaired	S-14	Free		
Conference-Approved Literature (CAL)	S-16	Free		
French Translations	S-16Fr	Free		
Spanish Translations	S-16Sp	Free		
Audio-Visual Material	S-16AV	Free		
Inside Al-Anon, Alateen Talk, and Al-Anon in Institutions Subscription form	S-53	Free		
The FORUM magazine Subscription form	S-54	Free		
Catalog: Al-Anon/Alateen CAL	S-15	Free		

COLUMN C TOTAL ______

Please add 5% for postage and handling on all orders.

NO C.O.D. ORDERS. PLEASE ALLOW 3 WEEKS FOR DELIVERY.

Make checks payable to: **AFG, Inc.**
P.O. Box 862, Midtown Station
New York, N.Y. 10018-0862

FOR ALATEEN

	CAT. #	PRICE PER	QUAN.	TOTAL COST
It's A Teenaged Affair	P-10	.15		
Twelve Steps and Twelve Traditions for Alateen	P-18	.60		
Youth and the Alcoholic Parent	P-21	.30		
If Your Parents Drink Too Much (Cartoon) 20/5.00 A †	P-22	.40		
Guide For Sponsors of Alateen Groups	P-29	Free		
Operation Alateen	P-30	.20		
Facts About Alateen	P-41	.20		
Alateen Sponsor To Sponsor	P-51	.45		
Moving On! From Alateen to Al-Anon	P-59	.45		
Alateen's 4th Step Inventory NEW	P-64	3.50		
Do's and Don'ts, Alateen 12/1.00 A †	M-9	100/7.00		
Just For Today, Alateen Wallet Card †	M-11	25/1.00		
Just For Today, Alateen Bookmark 12/1.00 A †	M-13	100/7.00		
Alateen Program Card 12/1.00 A †	M-18	100/7.00		
Do You Need Alateen? mimeo sheet	S-1	.15		
Alateen 10th Step Sheet	S-6	.15		
Alateen, Is It For You? 20 Questions †	S-20	100/2.00		
Alateen Discount Package —77 pieces	K-6	6.75		
Alateen Package—78 pieces includes B-3 book	K-7	10.25		
Alateen Newcomer's Packet 13 pieces	K-18	1.25		

See "Books" and Separate AUDIO-VISUAL orderblank (S-16AV) for additional Alateen material.

ADD ALL COLUMN TOTALS HERE

TOTAL + COLUMN D	
+ COLUMN C	
+ COLUMN B	
+ COLUMN A	
SUB TOTAL	
ADD 5% FOR HANDLING	
GRAND TOTAL	

Prices are in U.S. currency

IF AN ITEM HAS BEEN DISCONTINUED, we will substitute one that is similar in content, making the necessary adjustment in quantity.

†Bulk Discounts—items which are priced in multiples, e.g. 10/$1., are discounted at 10% on 1,000 or more.

Pamphlet Discounts—10% on 100 or more of one item.
20% discount on 1,000 or more of any one item.

CONTRIBUTIONS: Members only ______

PLEASE PRINT

SEND TO:
Name ______
P.O. Box ______
or Address ______
City ______ State ______ ZIP ______
Canadian Province ______
GROUP ID# ______
Name of Group ______
City Where Group Meets ______

Check total $	Date	Order #

DO NOT WRITE IN THIS SPACE

Appendix H

Substance Abuse Curriculum

Providing curriculum guides and suggestions for appropriate methodologies for classroom teachers is among the services that should be offered by school library media specialists. Collecting this information in the area of substance abuse can be a greater challenge than in the more traditional curriculum areas, especially when the need for accurate, up-to-date, and effective materials must be matched to the sense of inadequacy many faculty have in dealing with this topic. Research has been conducted to determine what is effective to use and the appropriate methodology to present the material, but the results are not often readily available.

Individual school districts have developed curricula for use in their district, and state departments of education have published suggested units for sharing the outcomes of using and abusing substances. It is often difficult to discover the existence of such guides or to secure copies, and little research has been conducted to assess the degree of success of commercially available curricula and even less of curricula that have been locally produced. Research on short-term results and long-term benefits is needed. This appendix includes information concerning the number of school districts engaged in substance abuse education, the degree of impact, suggested teaching strategies, and methods to select materials for use in the curriculum.

SUBSTANCE ABUSE EDUCATION IN SCHOOLS

Substance abuse research appears to have a somewhat narrow definition of substances. The published report of the Center for Education Statistics dated December 1987[1] states that "most local school districts take an active role in substance abuse education" with substance abuse referring to alcohol abuse, drug abuse, or both. Of those responding, 47 percent of the district officials believed that drug abuse in their districts had decreased in the last two years while 11 percent perceived an increase; 42 percent indicated no change. The statistics for alcohol abuse showed only 16 percent of the officials believed their district had a decrease, 29 percent perceived that there had been an increase in use, and 56 percent thought there had been no change. Large or urban districts are more likely to have substance abuse policies and to require substance abuse education than are smaller or rural districts. Indeed, there is a relationship between having a policy and having a requirement for substance abuse education. When an education program is required, it is a requirement at all instructional levels, not just secondary. Further,

> Substance abuse education may be offered in districts even if there is no specific district requirement for it. Thus at the senior high level, 96 percent of districts provide substance abuse education. Most typically, substance abuse education is part of the health curriculum (85 percent at the elementary level, 87 percent at the junior high level, and 83 percent at the senior high level). The next most common teaching method is through special assemblies and events; this is used by three-fourths of districts at the junior high and senior high levels.... Special assemblies and events are typically used by districts as a supplement to other methods of offering substance abuse education; only 1 percent of districts use them as their sole method of education. At the senior high level, substance abuse education is frequently offered through driver training as well (55 percent).[2]

Few districts reported having full-time staff directly assigned to substance abuse education, and almost one-third of the reporting districts had no staff with this responsibility. Most districts depended upon technical assistance from outside agencies including the state education agency, the state alcohol and drug abuse agency, and U.S. Department of Education regional centers.

Additional information was published in a report from the Office of Educational Research and Improvement of the U.S. Department of Education. A report to Congress and the White House gave the following statistics:

> Forty states currently mandate education about substance abuse. Twenty-eight of these specify that substance abuse prevention be taught in health education courses, while two states place this material in driver education courses. Thirty-two states have issued minimum substance abuse curricula standards, with five more planning to do so. Substance abuse education is a teacher certification requirement in all 11 states.[3]

Steps to increase the effectiveness of school-based substance abuse prevention education include:

- Begin with a clear policy stating that the school will *not* tolerate the use of tobacco, alcohol, and other illicit drugs by students. Communicate this policy to all concerned. Enforce it fairly and consistently for all students. Use it as the basis for prevention education efforts.

- Develop and enforce standards for all school personnel concerning their professional conduct and their roles in implementing prevention education.
- Select and implement a comprehensive K-12 substance abuse prevention curriculum, including teacher training and periodic evaluations of effectiveness.
- Incorporate into the curriculum ways to educate parents about substance abuse and involve them in prevention education.
- Provide accessible school- and community-based intervention and referral services to counsel and treat students with drug-related problems, and offer special educational arrangements where appropriate.
- Incorporate the no-use message into all school-based and school-sponsored activities and events, and encourage this practice in family and community activities as well.
- Involve parents and the entire community in all of the above steps through local Drug-Free Schools Advisory Councils and other activities.
- Develop a written understanding between school officials and law enforcement agencies regarding policies and procedures for intervention on school grounds in particular, and for cooperation and communication in general.
- Evaluate the whole comprehensive prevention program on a regular basis to ensure that it is meeting local needs, and use the results to make improvements and changes.[4]

Reports of substance abuse in schools have more often counted quantity rather than quality. Some reports of the impact of substance abuse education have been conducted. The results are reported below.

DEGREE OF IMPACT WITH SUBSTANCE ABUSE EDUCATION

More and more young people are being introduced to substance abuse at younger and younger ages. More and more, parents, communities, and the federal government, including the President, are advocating the need for strong substance abuse programs, and, as has been shown earlier, many education programs are in place. Yet, little research has been done to test the effect of any substance abuse program on young people, and few have been tested over a long enough period to confirm results over time.

Nancy Minix, in her article, "Drug and Alcohol Prevention Education,"[5] reports the results of research findings about alcohol and drug programs and the implications for education programs. Her premise is "that drug and alcohol experimentation and habitual use among the young is indeed a social problem, particularly in the early stages." She focuses on the following social areas:

Goal-setting skills (career and life-planning)

Anxiety/stress reduction skills

Decision-making skills

Self-esteem/self-concept development

Communication skills

Further, she points out that successful programs employ a team approach "combining comprehensive efforts of the school, the family, and the community." She summarizes that "the program should integrate not only instructional areas of concern but also the personal and maturational needs of the young person."

A study conducted in Canada queried nine-, twelve-, and fifteen-year-old students about health knowledge. Sheppard found that "for every grade level tested, knowledge scores on drugs were lower than any other health issue."[6]

Research has been conducted on the impact of particular programs. Tricker and Davis[7] evaluated two drug and alcohol programs, *Here's Looking at You, 2000* and *Starting Early*, in three Oregon school districts. While this study was conducted in elementary schools, the results related to teaching methods and preparation of teachers for the task will be reported below under that heading in the text that follows. However, "community and parental support for the drug and alcohol program was not clearly evident, and this was the aspect of the implementation that the administrators felt needed most improvement."[8]

The drug education package, "Double Take," was the subject of a study conducted in Great Britain by Eiser, Eiser, and Bocker.[9] This program consisted of two videos, teacher notes, and pupil exercises. The first video was based on a television series and showed peer pressure to encourage heroin use. The second video was more obviously didactic and less professionally prepared.

Results of this study indicated that little parental involvement had been sought in the choice of this substance abuse education program or in its implementation. Biology, English, social education, and health education were the courses chosen to cover drug education, and teachers evaluated the programs affirmatively. While teachers usually presented the program, some schools used the school nurse or a doctor or a health education officer rather than a classroom teacher. When teachers were asked what they believed to be the most effective way to persuade young people not to take drugs, they ranked as the highest factor "decision-making/life skills." These skills included "help them feel good about themselves, help them make decisions for themselves, help them talk about personal problems and worries, help them to practise saying no, and involve their parents in drug education."

Second ranking was given to "fear-arousal/role-play." This factor included "help them imagine being addicted to heroin, help them imagine being offered heroin, and make them really scared." Few teachers considered "make them really scared" as being at all helpful. The lowest-ranked factor was talking about other drugs including "talk about tobacco (at the same time as heroin), talk about alcohol, talk about tea and coffee, and talk about medicines."[10]

Reports from schools explain where substance abuse education is taught, but not whether it is better presented as a health issue, in biology, or in some other course. Research seems to confirm that parental and community involvement is essential.

As substance abuse programs become mandatory, as educators continue to invest their time and the school district's money to purchase substance abuse materials, measures need to be taken to assess the success of programs and results reported for the use of personnel in all school districts. Media specialists can take an active role in assisting with any research that can be conducted in the school district and to encourage the writing and distribution of results.

TEACHING METHODS FOR SUBSTANCE ABUSE EDUCATION

Daily, teachers choose the most effective methodology to present information for their students. Research has shown when media is more effective and when an alternate method is preferred or should be adopted. Media use has its own methodology for presentation. Only when an appropriate methodology is adhered to can the medium have the best possibility for successful learning and retention.

Student responses in the Sheppard study presented earlier seemed to indicate that films are "the least likely method of drug education while many people still insist it is the major source of drug education," and "movies and classes were generally rated fair to good; most classes (of those that had any) talked about only the bad effects of using drugs." The major teaching method was lecture or teacher-led class discussion.[11]

An interdisciplinary science-oriented curriculum "Alcohol and Drunkenness" was developed in Israel[12] to combat an increasing problem with excessive drinking in that country. This curriculum was described as a primary "preventive model" and dealt with Israeli high school students. Using a "decision-making" component, these non-conventional teaching methods included activities with "value-clarification." This goal-oriented curriculum, designed for affective and behavioral domains, had as its main objective a decline in a positive attitude toward excessive drinking and a "weakening of the desire and the readiness of the students to personally experience the excessive drinking of alcohol...." The main objective in the behavioral domain was to stop drinking altogether rather than "to ensure responsible, controlled, and moderate drinking." While this curriculum had been field-tested, full implementation had not been undertaken.

Parker[13] reported the test of a Drug Education Infusion Project proposal submitted as a method to implement guidelines presented in the Department of Education monograph, *Schools Without Drugs*. In developing the proposal, the researchers found that the use of the infusion strategy "helped to allay some of their sincerely felt shortcomings and to promote their feeling able to perform against a real felt need." Teachers wanted a direct method to combat the drug problem and "held rather realistic perceptions about how damaging, potentially dangerous and destructive the effects of the problem could yet become." They also noted that teachers were insecure about drug-specific knowledge. The researchers for this project overcame this through intensive workshops. Library media specialists can help teachers become more knowledgeable about drugs through in-service work in this area.

The researchers reported "the infusion strategy does promote program ownership by the classroom teacher," and that this strategy avoided both "detracting political and potentially negative accountability and targeting difficulties associated with other approaches." It halted the labelling of drug education as an "add-on." While the lack of information on "best method" of presenting substance abuse information makes it more difficult for the school library media specialist to suggest materials or methods for teaching in this area, it increases the need to keep current with the research on teaching and with the materials available on substance abuse.

An issue of *The Grantsmanship Center Whole Nonprofit Catalog* had a special section, "Focus on Drug Education," in its spring/summer 1990 issue. A debate was chronicled between Armand Mauss of Washington State University, who studied the Bainbridge School District program, and Clay Roberts, developer of *Here's Looking at You, 2000*, the curriculum used there. Mauss stated that

> ... the issue is finding out whether and which school prevention programs have a demonstrable impact on the actual use of drugs and alcohol by youth—not just on their knowledge, self-esteem, attitudes, refusal skills, etc. Until one or more school programs should prove effective in this regard, the main choice left to school administrators is simply one between more expensive and less expensive drug education programs.[14]

ASSESSMENT OF STUDENT LEARNING

The previous discussion has covered the evaluation of substance abuse education programs. Another facet of the use of such programs with students is the assessment of their knowledge about substance abuse and the information they have learned from the substance abuse curricula. "Concerning assessment, one principal is paramount: At all levels, substance abuse prevention material ought to be graded in the same way, and to the same standards, as other academic work."[15]

Regular testing and monitoring of student progress is recommended so that students do not perceive of the instruction as non-academic or extracurricular, either "playtime" or "fill-in, busy-work" time. It is further suggested that a comprehensive review be given at the end of third grade, when leaving elementary school at the end of fifth or sixth grade, when leaving junior high at the end of eighth or ninth grade, and before graduating from high school.

TEACHER PREPARATION

In order to plan effective in-service programs to acquaint teachers and parents with substance abuse issues, research shows the need for both short courses and longer sessions. Tricker and Davis found that teachers needed a shorter course when they were experienced in drug and alcohol education and only needed in-depth practical examination of curriculum materials. The longer in-service session should have a "more in-depth coverage of drug and alcohol issues with teaching instruction." This longer experience would provide a better foundation for the inexperienced teacher. Program coordinators in this study carried out the following assignments:

Planning and implementing training sessions

Coordinating wellness promotions and alcohol/drug abuse prevention in the district community

Providing in-service teacher training

Maintaining correspondence with trainees

Demonstrating lessons in schools

Identifying key demonstration teachers

Attempting to maintain communication with the district administration

Preparing materials, test sheets, and worksheets for teachers in all grades in every school[16]

In the Moore and Weiss study[17], teachers were given a fourteen-hour course in alcohol education. Teachers were then expected to be able to demonstrate greater teaching skills for teaching this subject than they needed for other classroom instruction.

SELECTION OF TEACHING MATERIALS FOR SUBSTANCE ABUSE EDUCATION

Before beginning the process of selecting a substance abuse prevention curriculum, the following steps are suggested.

- Determine the nature and extent of the drug problem in your area.

- Establish regular lines of communication among all parties who will play a role in your drug-prevention program—including teachers and other school staff, administrative and supervisory personnel, parents, community leaders, law enforcement officials, health professionals, and district and state officers.

- Obtain the commitment of all to support a firm no-use stance.

- Establish a means of regularly monitoring the extent and character of tobacco, alcohol, and other drug use, possession and distribution in your district, through the schools, and in cooperation with local law enforcement agencies.

- Develop a clear, concise policy against drug use in your school(s) that affirms a no-use philosophy, establishes definite sanctions, encourages both self-referral for help and drug-free lifestyles, and sets forth clear procedures for fair and firm enforcement.

- Communicate this policy to parents, students, staff and all others concerned, obtain formal assurance that they agree to it, and ensure that school personnel understand their roles and responsibilities under it.

- Plan your comprehensive school-based drug prevention program, and determine how the curriculum component should interact with the rest of the plan.

As you choose your curriculum:

- Commit to using a curriculum that conveys the no-use message.

- Commit to having a curriculum that is academically sound, that conveys accurate information, uses the best techniques, can be graded like any other subject, and can be coordinated with other disciplines at each grade level.

- Obtain the advice of teachers and parents, and consult with district and state officials regarding any special requirements.

- Develop specific criteria for desired content and outcomes, and for utility and flexibility.

- Analyze your needs, resources, and capabilities to determine whether it is best to design your own curriculum, or to apply your criteria to selecting or adapting a commercially available package.

- Control the process of selection through clear channels, and ensure lines of accountability. Don't let the process become unduly influenced by consultants or publishers' representatives.

- Make certain that adequate training in awareness of drug issues and knowledge of specific drug effects is provided for all school personnel, including administrative and supervisory people as well as teachers and support staff.

- Make certain that administrators and the superintendent will guarantee training support that is ongoing—not only money but time as well.

- Initiate the non-curricular components of the program, including parent and community support groups, business and professional support, drug-free activities, and an adequate network of intervention, referral, and treatment resources.

- Ensure that your curriculum reaches the entire student population.

- Provide for keeping parents informed about the curriculum and participating in it.[18]

Anderson, Fox, and Salmon[19] cite the passage of the Drug-Free Schools and Community Act of 1987 for the renewed and increased attention on drug and alcohol abuse by students. They have stated the considerations for the selection of a curriculum for the schools and suggest that the choice should match the purpose and philosophy of the program. Choosing a district-wide curriculum may take more time. The need for a greater number of previewers from the varied grade levels and the higher cost for the program may inhibit a speedy implementation. Smaller, less expensive packages may be preferable.

The criteria for choice of curriculum reflect standard criteria that are applied to all materials to be purchased for use by students. They are repeated here because they represent the emphasis of these authors who divide their criteria into "content, instructional, and physical properties." In the area of content, the program should have modules at each grade level or the material should fit into a comprehensive scope and sequence. All curriculum approaches should be based on recent research concerning age appropriateness and the integration of cognitive, affective, coping, and behavioral approaches. As with all materials, information should be accurate and up-to-date.

Clearly defined goals and instructional objectives are essential in the cognitive, affective, and behavioral areas. Materials should be free of sex, race, or ethnic stereotypes and not time-bound.

With the instructional properties, attention should be paid to the difficulty of the content and its relationship to the grade level. Materials should fit into the school's curriculum. Some evidence should be given that the materials are effective and that they attract and maintain student interest. Preferably, materials should be field-tested in a variety of schools.

Physical properties include ease of preview and purchase, the availability of teacher training, the completeness of teacher manuals, and cost-effectiveness. Support materials such as films, pamphlets, or games should be relevant, targeted, and integral to the curriculum content. Further, suggestions should be given for parent education and involvement. As cited earlier, programs with little or no community involvement are less effective than others.

The developers of *Here's Looking at You, 2000* cite the following criteria for measuring the potential effectiveness of any drug education curriculum.

- Is the curriculum based on current research about why young people use drugs?
- Does the curriculum provide more than information?
- Does the curriculum begin early and is it ongoing?
- Does the curriculum focus on "gateway drugs" (nicotine, alcohol, marijuana)?
- Can the curriculum be easily incorporated into a total approach to health education and welfare?
- Does the curriculum take a positive approach?
- Does the curriculum have a clear "no use" message?[20]

Several suggested criteria have been reported in their entirety rather than being synthesized. It was decided that media specialists would prefer to review each suggested criteria list and then develop their own.

In reading research, media specialists may wish to have guidelines to assess the quality of the evaluation literature. One researcher considered the process of evaluating education programs and proposed basic principles to be used in evaluating the evaluations of drug education programs. These included:

- Evaluations should include data from both control and experimental groups.
- Evaluations should also include data that show before-and-after measures.
- Evaluations should show comparability between control and experimental groups.
- Evaluations should use longitudinal data, not repeated cross-sectional data.
- Evaluations should focus on *behavior.*
- Evaluations should distinguish between impact on one kind of drug use and impact on another kind of drug use.
- Evaluations should focus on the most crucial age period for a kid.
- Evaluations should provide school people and school boards with the kind of evidence they need to make cost-benefit assessments.
- The value of the peer review process should be emphasized when evaluating published research.[21]

Discussion in *Drug Prevention Curriculum* covers whether to buy, adapt, or develop programs for substance abuse prevention education. It is reported that some states such as California have very detailed regulations and require very specific content and procedures. Some states are currently in the process of developing or revising substance abuse prevention curricula guidelines. Twenty-five states have adopted commercial or state-developed curricula. In some states, such as Pennsylvania, the adopted curricula are mandated for all districts. In others, such as Texas, the curricula may be chosen from a range of approved selections. In Virginia, the adopted curricula is approved, but not mandated.

When packaged curricula are available, the programs can be very expensive, up to $6,000 for materials and teachers' and students' manuals. If training sessions are suggested, transportation and consultants may increase this price. Many districts may adapt curricula from other locations to their needs. Some school districts join with law enforcement agencies to produce and implement their prevention curriculum. Whether commercially purchased or locally developed, the suggested criteria include:

- Ease of use.
- Appropriate and clearly defined goals and objectives.
- Longevity and regular updating.
- Flexibility and adaptability to different teaching styles and needs.
- Completeness, timeliness, and accuracy of materials.
- Ability to be integrated with other subjects.
- Proven track record of success (if purchased from a publisher).
- Readily available customer service (if purchased).
- Cost-effectiveness—considering published materials plus training and other prevention program components.[22]

Mauss reported two studies, Project SMART in the Kansas City area and Project ALERT. Both projects focus on changing the perception of children that using and abusing substances is not "cool." Since most children do not use most drugs, a student can focus on dealing with peers by learning refusal skills and skills to cope with difficult social situations.

The RAND Corporation study of junior high school students in twenty California and Oregon schools tested Project Alert.[23] This substance abuse teaching method is behaviorally based. Students are given opportunities to identify pro-drug pressures from peers and to develop and practice strategies to counter these pressures and their need to fit in with the group. The results of this research points out that this method reduced cigarette smoking among adolescents who had experimented with cigarettes but were not regular smokers, but that it did not prevent non-smokers from trying cigarettes for the first time. However, it had no real effect on drinking.

The RAND Corporation has been funded for a longitudinal study tracing the students through high school. Media specialists can search the literature for findings of these two projects so that successful measures can be reported to their teachers.

The role of the media specialist in substance abuse prevention curricula remains an important one as teachers, counselors, administrators, parents, and the community seek to provide appropriate, accurate, and relevant information for students. Assisting these educators in the choice and implementation of an effective substance abuse program will make a major contribution to the school.

NOTES

[1]"District Efforts in Substance Abuse Education," in *OERI Bulletin.* (Washington, D.C.: Center for Education Statistics, 1987).

[2]Ibid.

[3]*Drug Prevention Curriculum: A Guide to Selection and Implementation.* (Washington, D.C.: Office of Educational Research and Improvement, U.S. Department of Education, 1988) 3.

[4]Ibid., 3-4.

[5]Nancy A. Minix, "Drug and Alcohol Prevention Education: A Developmental Social Skills Approach," *The Clearing House for the Contemporary Education in Middle & Secondary Schools* 61 (December 1987): 162-65.

[6]Margaret A. Sheppard, Michael S. Goodstadt, and Beverley Williamson. "Drug Education: Why We Have So Little Impact," *Journal of Drug Education* 15 (1985) :1-5.

[7]Ray Tricker, and Lorraine G. Davis, "Implementing School Drug and Alcohol Curricula: A Descriptive Evaluation." *Techniques: A Journal of Remedial Education and Counseling* 3 (October 1987) :281-93.

[8]Ibid., 290.

[9]Christine Eiser, J. Richard Eiser, and Martin Bocker. "Teachers' Evaluations of 'Life-Skills' Approach to Drugs Education," *Educational Research* 30 (November 1988): 202-10.

[10]Ibid., 208.

[11]Sheppard, Goodstadt, and Williamson, " Drug Education," 3.

[12]Michael Moore, and Shoshana Weiss, "Alcohol and Drunkenness – A Newly Developed Curricular Unit as a Model for Drug-Education, Science Oriented Curricular Programs," *Journal of Drug Education* 15 (1985): 263-71.

[13]Reese Parker. "Perceived Strengths of Drug Education Infusion Strategies and Support from Funding Sources and School Districts" (Paper presented at the Annual Meeting of the Western Psychological Association, Washington, D.C., U.S. Department of Education, 30 April 1989).

[14]"Focus on Drug Education," *The Grantsmanship Center Whole Nonprofit Catalog* 12 (spring/summer 1990).

[15]*Drug Prevention Curriculum*, 27.

[16]Tricker and Davis, "Implementing School Drug and Alcohol Curricula," 286.

[17]Moore and Weiss, "Alcohol and Drunkenness," 265-66.

[18]*Drug Prevention Curriculum*, vii-viii.

[19]Patricia Anderson, S. Lynn Fox, and Jennifer R. Salmon, *Curricula and Programs for Drug and Alcohol Education*, (Portland, OR: Northwest Regional Educational Laboratory, 1987).

[20]"Criteria for Effective Drug Education Curricula." Flyer accompanying brochure for *Here's Looking at You, 2000.* (Curriculum program, see annotation, p. 154.)

[21]"Focus on Drug Education," *Whole Nonprofit Catalog.*

[22]*Drug Prevention Curriculum*, 41-42.

[23]Ibid.

SUBSTANCE ABUSE CURRICULA

Clear Choices for High School. Tampa, FL: The C. E. Mendez Foundation, 1989 and 1990. $35.00. Workbooks $.50 ea.

Lessons have been developed to be incorporated into specific subject areas. Lessons meet the objectives for the subject, but are designed to be used in conjunction with standard curricula in the areas of American history, world history, law, driver's education, nutrition, and peer leadership. Each lesson emphasizes the consequences and costs of substance abuse. The goal is to "arm students with the facts they need to refuse drugs during a time when they are strongly influenced by peer pressure."

Choices and Challenges. Tampa, FL: The C. E. Mendez Foundation, rev. 1988. $35.00. Workbooks $.50 ea.

A curriculum designed for parents of pre-teens and teenagers, this four-week course of two-hour sessions is designed to prepare adults for active parenting and to educate them about the choices their children will face, offering ways to reduce the risk of substance abuse by teenagers. The first session focuses on alcohol and drug use in present-day society. The second session includes information on street drugs, adolescent development, and the role of the family in helping teens develop self-esteem. The third week's session focuses on drug information, prevention strategies, and how to recognize and to confront, more effectively, substance abuse. The final session discusses guidelines for effective alternatives and ways to help teens live healthier and happier lives.

Cone, Richard, and Barbara Werner Sayad. **Choices: A Substance Abuse Prevention Program for Junior High Students.** Deerfield Beach, FL: Health Communications, Inc., 1984. 79p.

A brief introduction provides some suggestions for teaching the course. The ten lessons in this small paperback book include "The Big Hustle—Advertising," " 'With Friends Like This....'—Peer Pressure," "The Choice Is Yours—Personal Values," "The Dope on Drugs—Drug Content," "No, Thank You—A Lesson in Self Assertion," "A Right to Choose—More Self Assertion," "De-Energize Me—Stress Reduction," and "Celebrate Life—Values Clarification and Celebration." Each short lesson has one or more suggested activities, supplemental related activities, and a vocabulary list. While this is called "A Bilingual (Spanish & English) Program Developed by The Joint Educational Project University of California," only the handout materials and some phrases to be placed on the chalkboard have been translated into Spanish.

Drugs: A Deadly Game.

Material for this Youth Awareness/Prevention Campaign was distributed to each of the 407 local councils of the Boy Scouts of America and is available from Boy Scouts of America, Magazine Division, 1325 Walnut Hill Lane, P.O. Box 152079, Irving, Texas 75015-2079, telephone (214) 580-2000. Designed as a multi-media, multi-faceted drug education experience to stimulate discussion in small-group or classroom settings, their "market-basket of easily digestible facts that will get children talking—and learning—about the dangers of drug use and abuse" includes a Drug Abuse Material Kit ($32). Items may be ordered separately including 100 Drug Abuse 18-page, full-color brochure with five accompanying teacher's guides designed to reinforce the positive values of staying drug free ($16), a videotape with accompanying brochure to use in classroom or with youth groups ($16), and a 23" x 32" poster (2 sides) from the centerfold of the brochure (varying prices from $5 unmounted to $700 for 100 laminated/metal edged posters). This information is also available in Spanish.

Freeman, Shelley MacKay. **From Peer Pressure to Peer Support: Alcohol/Drug Prevention through Group Process, A Curriculum for Grades 7-12.** Minneapolis, MN: The Johnson Institute, 1989. 325p. $59.95. ISBN 0-935908-48-X. (GR 7-12)

As the title implies, this curriculum is an attempt to turn peer pressure into peer support. The producers of this curriculum state that experience with this curriculum has shown improvement in academic work. "Teachers see improved student self-management skills and greater active participation in the learning process." The curriculum is designed as a systems approach and is structured around the group process. It provides for small group interaction through three developmental stages, building trust, resolving conflicts, and becoming a productive working group. Students are simultaneously learning basic life skills. Because this is a systems approach, cooperative methods of instruction help expand the teaching through identification, early intervention, referral, counseling, support groups, and involvement of the school community. The curriculum includes ready-to-duplicate-and-use activity pages for homeroom or health classes and a suggested lesson plan format. Training on how to use the curriculum is available from the Johnson Institute.

Here's Looking at You, 2000.® Developed by Roberts, Fitzmahan & Associates, 1986. (GR 7-9 and 10-12)

Originally developed for the Educational Service District #121 in Seattle, Washington, under the supervision of Comprehensive Health Education Foundation (CHEF), this program is presently available from CHEF. A variety of materials are available as kits or may be purchased as individually priced items: $1.00 for message posters, $4.00 for transparencies, $25.00 for each teacher's guide, and $180.00 for videocassettes. Using loose-leaf notebook format, this curriculum is designed with opportunities to involve parents, law enforcement officers, counselors, and community organizations. The scope and sequence are divided among "information," "skills," and "bonding to school and family." Part I, "Before You Begin," presents risk factors, ground rules, resource list, speakers, student measures, cross-age teaching, and a teacher checklist. A curriculum chart, student objectives, and suggestions for beginning and ending lessons are presented. Part II includes lesson plans with objectives listed, the resources needed beyond what is offered in the kit, and worksheets. For older students, Part III includes "The Yellow Pages," a resource supplement.

Newsweek. **On the Drug Crisis: Kids and Cocaine.**

Developed as a public service program in cooperation with McDonald's, this booklet closely resembles a copy of *Newsweek*. A teacher's guide accompanies the student booklet.

Index by Authors and Titles

Index by Subject Headings

Index of Media Type by Subject: General Collection